Whiteness at Work

Whiteness at Work

Edited by

Michael A. Moreno,
Kathryn Quinn–Sánchez
and Michele Shaul

Cambridge
Scholars
Publishing

Whiteness at Work

Edited by Michael A. Moreno, Kathryn Quinn–Sánchez
and Michele Shaul

This book first published 2020

Cambridge Scholars Publishing

Lady Stephenson Library, Newcastle upon Tyne, NE6 2PA, UK

British Library Cataloguing in Publication Data
A catalogue record for this book is available from the British Library

ISBN (10): 1-5275-5768-5
ISBN (13): 978-1-5275-5768-0

Contents

INTRODUCTION

MICHAEL A. MORENO,
KATHRYN QUINN–SÁNCHEZ
AND MICHELE SHAUL

The name on your résumé. The way you style your hair. The sound of your voice. The wording and punctuation you use in emails. The length of your commute. These are just a handful of the considerations that researchers have found disproportionately burdensome to people of color pursuing employment and advancement in the workplace.

This is, of course, by design. It is whiteness at work.

Though American mythology tells us that hard work pays off, fewer and fewer Americans are buying that line. The Pew Research Center found in 2014 that 38 percent of its survey respondents agreed with the statement that "hard work and determination are no guarantee of success for most people." That was 8 percentage points higher than when Pew asked the question two decades earlier. Though a Gallup survey in 2019 found that only 29 percent of respondents said that working hard and playing by the rules will not guarantee you'll achieve the American Dream, that was 5 percentage points higher than when Gallup asked the same question a decade earlier and 16 percentage points higher than when they asked it at the turn of the century. Nonwhite respondents were even less optimistic than White respondents; 37 percent said the American Dream was unattainable. The myth, it seems, is losing its grip on American workers, who are ever more cognizant of discrimination and income inequality and the systems and policies that perpetuate them.

You don't have to be a pollster, a human-resources professional or a scholar to know that who gets hired, how they're managed, and whether and when they're selected for promotion has little to do with merit. You need only have applied for or had a job. You've seen how academic pedigree, family connections and political ties influence hiring decisions. You've witnessed how workplace disputes are adjudicated and workload and credit are distributed. You've recognized the tokenism, prejudice and ostracizing that results in attrition of colleagues of color. You know that the myth of meritocracy comforts some and gaslights others. You know that no workplace is neutral.

In this book, we present a series of personal essays that explore the role of whiteness in the workplace.

What Do We Mean By "Whiteness"?

Whiteness is a social construct devised to categorize people—to create a privileged ingroup and disempowered outgroup. There is no biological basis of race, but the concept of whiteness has, as Halley et al. put it in their book *Seeing White: An Introduction to White Privilege and Race*, "helped to solidify the social power of the economic elite by encouraging poor and working-class people who became white to see themselves as a part of an ingroup with the elite, a group that excluded and subordinated people of color." In her 2011 essay "White Fragility," Robin DiAngelo, who later penned a book by the same name, described whiteness as "dynamic, relational, and operating at all times and on myriad levels." Whiteness is ubiquitous and for that reason invisible. It is seen as normal, default and ordinary.

Throughout American history, various ethnic groups have acquired whiteness and the status and privileges it affords. The Irish, for example, were granted whiteness after previously being considered a lesser race and being subject to "No Irish Need Apply" advertisements for jobs in the nineteenth and early twentieth centuries. Writing in the *New York Times*, Nell Irvin Painter, author of the book *The History of White People*, explains: "Then new waves of poor Eastern and Southern European immigrants arrived, inspiring new racial classifications: the 'Northern Italian' race, the 'Southern Italian' race, the 'Eastern European Hebrew' race, and so on. Their heads were measured and I.Q.s assessed to quantify (and, later, to deny) racial difference. They were all white, members of white races. But, like the Irish before them, the Italians and Jews and Greeks were classified as inferior white races." Jews, who face bigotry and hate crimes like other outgroups do, have been categorized as White since the Naturalization Act of 1790, and "[t]here's no doubt that the vast majority of American Jews live with what we would call white privilege," Jonathan Greenblatt, the CEO of the Anti-Defamation League, told *The Atlantic*. He continued: "They aren't looked at twice when they walk into a store. They aren't looked at twice by someone in uniform. … That obviously isn't a privilege that people of color have the luxury of enjoying."

Whiteness even has been granted, sort of, to those who do not necessarily pass for White. Eric Liu, who directs the Aspen Institute's

Citizenship & American Identity Program, noted in a 2014 column for CNN.com that "Asian Americans who've achieved in visible ways have been granted 'honorary white' status (wanted or not)." Writing in *The Guardian* about the Trump administration's move to no longer categorize people with Middle Eastern and North African origins as White for the U.S. Census, columnist Arwa Mahdawi explains, "[W]hiteness has always been a fluid category. Whiteness isn't a biological fact, rather it is a sort of members-only club that has rewritten its entry requirements over the years." It would be wrong, however, to interpret this fluidity as meaning that anyone, regardless of appearance, might be granted entrance to the whiteness club. Whiteness is about exclusion, not inclusion. We see this, especially, in the workplace.

Discrimination is "Distressingly Uniform"

Populations that have not been granted whiteness experience discrimination in the workplace at different rates and in different ways. Below, we will look at a sampling of evidence for and variation in discrimination at the application, interview, hiring and advancement stages. Though we are starting with the application stage, we want to emphasize that school segregation, housing discrimination, and other systems of oppression set the stage for what plays out during the application process and thereafter.

While job applicants of color might want to believe that hiring discrimination is a thing of the past, that simply is not true. (This may be especially disappointing for first-generation college grads of color hopeful that their academic credentials will afford them acceptance and greater opportunities than were afforded to their parents.) Princeton University researchers conducted a meta-analysis of all available field experiment studies of discrimination at the point of hire from 1989 through 2015 and found no reduction in the rate of discrimination against Black people and only a "marginally statistically significant" reduction in discrimination against Latinos. Writing in the *Proceedings of the National Academy of Sciences*, the researchers concluded, "we find the persistence of discrimination at a distressingly uniform rate." Studies focusing on the specifics of the hiring process show how this discrimination happens.

Reading Résumés

Over the years, there have been many studies demonstrating that the name on your résumé affects your chances of getting a callback after applying for a job. Though there's a lot of variation in study design, with some researchers choosing names that sound decidedly Black and decidedly White and others choosing names that are ambiguous, and thus variation in the results, experts agree that your name matters, because it conveys information not only about your race but also your socioeconomic class, which brings us to your home address.

David Phillips, a researcher at the University of Notre Dame, reported in 2018 in the *Journal of Human Resources* that managers screening applicants for low-wage jobs are less likely to call Black applicants who have longer commutes. "In many cities, urban revitalization has also led to increased rents, gentrification, and movement of low-income, minority groups away from jobs," Phillips explained in the *Harvard Business Review*. "So, when a low-wage employer avoids an employee due to their commute, that penalty disproportionately affects groups facing other disadvantages."

On top of that, the actual contents of your résumé, for example the section on extracurricular activities and community service, can work against you. A study by Harvard University researchers in 2017 found that both Black and Asian job applicants who "whiten" their résumés double their chances of getting called for interviews. And lest you think that companies that claim a commitment to diversity are a cut above, in fact, "Employers claiming to be pro-diversity discriminated against résumés with racial references just as much as employers who didn't mention diversity at all in their job ads."

Note that the studies we have described here say nothing about qualifications. They demonstrate that people of color face discrimination at the application stage that has nothing to do with their skills or experience. To underscore this point, we will share one more finding: The late Devah Pager at Northwestern University in 2003 found that employers are more likely to consider White men with criminal records than Black men with clean records. That alone speaks volumes.

Negotiating Pay

The gap in pay between men and women (about 20 cents in 2017) is getting more and more attention by policymakers, the media and hiring managers. Disparities along racial and ethnic lines are less often discussed but even more extreme. It should come as no surprise to you that White men earn more than Black and Latino men and women of all backgrounds. According to the National Women's Law Center, Latinx women made 53 cents to every dollar White men made in 2017. Black women made 61 cents, and Asian women made 85 cents. There are several intersecting beliefs and behaviors that contribute to the perpetuation of these and other disparities in compensation, and we'll touch on only a few below, but whiteness, without question, is at the core.

After job seekers of color do get to the offer table, they must contend with the salary negotiation process. In a series of three studies, researchers at the Massachusetts Institute of Technology took a close look at the role race plays in those negotiations, and the findings are illustrative. In the first study, participants evaluated the résumés of job applicants and judged Black candidates as less likely to negotiate. In the second study, the researchers zeroed in on racially biased study participants, who indicated that they expected Black applicants to be less aggressive during negotiations. In the third study, the researchers had the evaluators interact with the applicants and found that, though the Black and White applicants negotiated comparably, the White evaluators perceived Black applicants as being pushier, which resulted in lower salary offers. It seems, as the saying goes, Black candidates are damned if they do (negotiate) and damned if they don't.

The relative success of Asians in America often is used by pundits and politicians on the right to argue that pay and other disparities affecting Black and Latino workers are of their own making—that they would have successes similar to Asians' if only they'd raise their kids right, if only they'd prioritize education, if only they'd work hard. This argument has been bolstered by the popularization, by those on the left as well, of the "tiger mom" archetype. It is, after all, reassuring to tell yourself that proper rearing and educational attainment will help you or your children overcome an inherently unfair system. Research by Nathaniel Hilger at Brown University, however, found in 2017 that, though the model-minority myth alleges that Asian upward mobility is a product of scholastic achievement, in fact, Americans simply have become less racist toward Asians, which has allowed them to, among other things, close the wage gap with White workers. Nonetheless, Asian-American white-collar professionals are the least likely group to be selected for management positions.

Advancement

Given what we know about the discrimination faced and burdens carried by workers of color, only a sampling of which we've described above, it should come as no surprise that few manage to reach positions of power in their respective fields.

Fortune magazine, which tracks diversity in the ranks and in the C-suite of Fortune 500 companies, reported in 2017 that 72 percent of top officials were White men. The population of CEOs is even more White and male. A

2016 survey by the Hispanic Association on Corporate Responsibility found that about 4 percent of executive officers at Fortune 500 firms are Hispanic and that Hispanics held just over 7 percent of board seats. Importantly, 99 percent of those Hispanic executives are men. Black CEOs are even scarcer: In 2018, there were only three (in total) at Fortune 500 firms.

Leadership positions in the nonprofit sector also are held overwhelmingly by White people (almost half of whom are White women, by the way). One of the usual excuses for the whiteness of nonprofit executives is that there simply aren't enough diverse candidates for such positions. Yet despite the development of leadership programs specifically aimed at developing talent of color for those positions, their numbers on the job haven't been increasing, according to a report by the Building Movement Project. "The results call into question the common assumption that to increase the diversity of nonprofit leaders, people of color need more training," said Frances Kunreuther, BMP's co-director. Another myth is that people of color are less likely than White people to aspire to leadership positions at nonprofits. On the contrary, BMP found that people of color were 10 percentage points more likely to say they want those jobs than White people. "The findings point to a new narrative. To increase the number of people of color leaders, the nonprofit sector needs to address the practices and biases of those governing nonprofit organizations," Kunreuther said.

In the public sector, things are better but not equitable. Nonwhite civil servants make up 38 percent of the federal workforce, which is close to their share of the U.S. population. However, according to the U.S. Office of Personnel Management, in 2018 they held only 21 percent of senior executive jobs. Importantly, the 2018 OPM report doesn't include the Trump administration's numbers, "but no one expects things to improve under this president. Quite the opposite," wrote Washington Post columnist Joe Davidson.

Uncompensated Labor

Whiteness affects the day-to-day lives of workers of color in ways that those who consider themselves White are unlikely to recognize. Here is just a handful of examples:

- The Good Hair Study in 2017 found that White women, who make up about one-third of managers, demonstrate, more so than any other group polled, both implicit and explicit bias against textured hair and believe it to be "less professional than smooth hair."

- Candy Lee, a professor at the Medill journalism school at Northwestern University, examined how voice characteristics affect perceived leadership capabilities. She wrote in *Forbes*, "My research showed that—based solely on audio—a white man is the preferred leader over a black man, a white woman and a black woman."
- In a study describing Black women's experiences with promotion opportunities, Marlese Durr and Adia M. Harvey Wingfield wrote: "They speak of performance weariness in verbal and nonverbal communicative interaction-exchanges with white colleagues. Many simply state that they feel they are in a 'parade,' being judged for appearance, personal decorum, communication skills, and emotion management in addition to productivity."

It is whiteness that cloaks the above described emotional, uncompensated labor.

Reporting Discrimination

Workers of color who experience racism on the job and hope to get some sort of restitution or resolution have an uphill battle. Many employers require that disputes be handled through private arbitration, and discrimination cases fare worse than other types of cases in that venue. Though the Civil Rights Act of 1964 established the U.S. Equal Employment Opportunity Commission to investigate complaints, the agency is not a safety net. Maryam Jameel and Joe Yerardi at the Center for Public Integrity reported in early 2019 that, of the 100,000 workplace-discrimination cases closed by the EEOC and its partner agencies each year, fewer than one-fifth of them result in some sort of financial compensation or workplace change. Upon concluding their analysis of seven years of data, the journalists wrote: "What emerged is a picture of a system that routinely fails workers." Indeed, the backlog of cases is long, and many workers pursuing EEOC cases simply give up. Importantly, discrimination cases are especially difficult because the burden of proof is on the employee, but the employer holds the keys to personnel files. "Many workers who sue—generally permitted only after they seek assistance from the EEOC or its partner agencies—file in federal court, where workplace discrimination cases number less than 15 percent of annual EEOC claims," Jameel and Yerardi reported.

Whiteness Controls the Narrative

Most of the statistics and studies mentioned in this introduction have been reported within the past few years by the media. While that might lead you to think that the press does a reasonably decent job of exposing the effects of whiteness on workers of color, that is and isn't the case. Yes, one-off studies sometimes make headlines. That's how we found a lot of the ones we've described here. But we rarely hear in-depth discussions on cable news or talk radio about how the compounding effects of whiteness affect workers of color on a day-to-day basis or over a lifetime. You don't need a crystal ball to predict that drive-by, shallow reporting won't have sustained or meaningful effects on workers.

You might feel inclined to attribute the lack of comprehensive and contextualized reporting on workers of color on the whiteness of newsrooms themselves, and, again, you'd be right, but only partially. In 2018, the Pew Research Center found that newsrooms are both more white and more male than typical American workplaces. Some 77 percent of newsroom staffers were White (compared with 65 percent of all U.S. workers), and 61 percent were male (compared with 53 percent of all U.S. workers). These numbers align with estimates by the American Society of News Editors, which in 1978 pledged to pursue parity with national averages and has so far failed to achieve that goal.

The whiteness of political reporting is undeniable and concerning. Case in point: Farai Chideya of Harvard's Shorenstein Center on Media, Politics and Public Policy asked 15 news outlets about who made up their 2016 presidential election reporting teams. Though only four outlets responded in full, the data Chideya received were revealing. The team covering the election for the *New York Times*, for example, was 90 percent White. Numbers like that should worry workers of color. Politicians, after all, are the ones who write, vote on and sign legislation affecting workers' rights, pay, healthcare and protections.

When whiteness blinds the watchdogs, the consequences aren't distributed evenly. Earlier, we mentioned that many racial-discrimination complaints brought to the EEOC end up being abandoned by the complainants. One reason for that is the case backlog; it can take months to get a response from the agency. The backlog exists, in part, because, though the EEOC's responsibilities have expanded over the decades, its budget has not kept pace. Today, there are simply too few agents available to investigate all the complaints the agency receives. Though the backlog affects all complainants, it hurts Black workers disproportionately, because their reports of racial discrimination make up a quarter of all EEOC cases. It's worth considering what the news coverage of the EEOC and what the agency's backlog might look like today had White men been the ones on the receiving end of racial epithets, threats and violence in the workplace.

Importantly, the media allow politicians to set the national tone by giving them a platform for their ideas, even when they are wrongheaded or, as we have seen in the case of Donald Trump, downright dangerous. The workplace is not immune from infectious invective. When the president spews anti-immigrant rhetoric on the White House lawn before a gaggle of reporters, news outlets give him a platform and then repeat his hateful rhetoric on a loop. We can't act surprised when attacks on immigrant workers increase or, worse, a gunman mows down immigrants and Americans at a Walmart. Whiteness determines what is newsworthy, consequences be damned.

In addition to having the power to give dangerous people the bully pulpit, the media also have the power to erase marginalized perspectives when it suits whiteness. When the #MeToo hashtag in 2017 blew up on Twitter, in response to a post by actress Alyssa Milano, millions of women shared their stories of sexual harassment and assault and expressed solidarity with other victims. Tarana Burke, however, panicked. "I felt a sense of dread, because something that was part of my life's work was going to be co-opted and taken from me and used for a purpose that I hadn't originally intended," Burke told the *New York Times*. You see, Burke already had coined "me too" and had used it in her campaigns for abuse victims. But the Milano tweet was the talk of the town. Later, Milano credited Burke on "Good Morning America" and elsewhere, but, as they say, you cannot unring a bell, and most Americans will go on without associating Me Too with Tarana Burke.

Another example of erasure has to do with Democratic calls for Trump's impeachment. U.S. Rep. Maxine Waters of California, who is Black and often the target of the president's racist insults, began calling for impeachment in early 2017. U.S. Rep. Al Green of Texas, who is also Black, filed articles of impeachment in July 2019 in response to Trump's racist attacks on U.S. Reps. Alexandria Ocasio–Cortez of New York, Ilhan Omar of Minnesota, Ayanna Pressley of Massachusetts and Rashida Tlaib of Michigan. (All women of color, they are often called "The Squad" by the president and the press. Trump said they should "go back" to their ancestral homelands, despite the fact that all are American citizens, and three were born in the U.S.) Once House Speaker Nancy Pelosi announced the formal impeachment inquiry on Sept. 24, 2019, the one that Waters and Green had been calling for all along, CNN's Dana Bash in a Sunday feature showcased four White congresswomen as "unlikely leaders on impeachment." Bash said on air: "Backing an impeachment inquiry is risky political business for these congresswomen," who had won election in "mostly Trump territory."

Though newsroom diversity has improved slightly over the years, and younger newsroom employees are more diverse than older ones, this isn't just a numbers game. To begin with, minority employees have many obvious incentives for upholding whiteness. As Kathleen McElroy, director of the School of Journalism at the University of Texas at Austin, makes plain in a column for the Poynter Institute, a journalism training organization, "throwing bodies at journalism's diversity problem hasn't worked." McElroy argues that the "longstanding yet flawed journalistic tenet" of objectivity is at the core of the newsroom diversity problem. "Both sides" journalism, as it is practiced in newsrooms across the country today, undermines justice. Sometimes one side is flat-out wrong, and sometimes one side is disproportionately wronged. Performative neutrality aids oppressors.

Swimming in It

Many of the stories in this collection were written by people who've been employed in a variety of fields over the years but who today work in the education sector, including the editors, so we'd like to say just a bit about whiteness in education.

We ask you to first consider the denazification of Germany after the Allied victory of World War II. Nazis were removed from positions of power and their various organizations were disbanded. The effort included physical scrubbing, too. "Stone swastikas were chiseled off the façades of buildings, Nazi insignia were taken down from flagpoles, and, in towns and cities across Germany, streets and squares named after [Adolf] Hitler reverted to their previous designations," writes Richard J. Evans in *Foreign Affairs*. Nonetheless, to this day the vestiges of ethnic cleansing remain emblazoned on schools named after party members and supporters. Imagine how Jewish students, teachers and staff members, among others who during the war would have been considered biologically inferior, must feel walking into schools honoring war criminals who exterminated their ancestors. It's an unreasonable ask, really, and an unnecessary one. And yet certain segments of local communities remain resistant to efforts to name those schools after those who were not complicit in genocide.

Meanwhile, here in America, there are upwards of 100 schools that still bear the names of members of the Confederacy, according to the Southern Poverty Law Center. We expect Black children, teachers and staffers, and others from groups that were considered inferior by White slaveholders, to do their best work under the banner of Robert E. Lee, Jefferson Davis and

"Stonewall" Jackson. Again, it is an unreasonable ask, really, and an unnecessary one. But whiteness prevails.

Even at American public schools that bear the names of true role models, children of color are unlikely to be taught by teachers from backgrounds like their own. According to the National Center for Education Statistics, in the 2015–2016 school year, 80 percent of teachers were White, 9 percent were Hispanic, 7 percent were Black, 2 percent were Asian, and 1 percent were of two or more races. This is concerning because study after study has shown that students of color who have teachers of the same race are more likely to graduate from high school and enroll in college. More disturbing, though, are the studies showing that Black and Brown children are perceived by White adults as older and more mature than their White peers of the exact same age, which explains why even the youngest of students of color face harsher penalties, including suspensions and expulsions.

At colleges and universities, where several of this collection's authors work, the protection of whiteness is most obvious when faculty and administrators defend White supremacist ideas and behaviors under the guise of protecting free speech and academic freedom. They call townhall meetings after hate crimes on campus but fail to expel or otherwise sanction the perpetrators. They arrange anti-discrimination workshops but do not require employees to attend them. They say they are striving for inclusion but allow neo-Nazis to assemble and spew hate speech on campus. They claim to prioritize diversity in hiring but fail to make the institutional changes required to retain faculty of color.

Times of Crisis Shine a Light on Injustice

The COVID-19 pandemic and nationwide protests against extrajudicial killings of Black people by police officers have provoked a barrage of formal statements by companies, organizations and institutions about their commitments to the safety and well-being of their customers and workers and to racial justice. What remains to be seen is whether those statements will result in meaningful changes.

Black, Latino and Native American communities have been disproportionately affected by COVID-19 in large part because of longstanding inequities rooted in racism: air pollution, segregated housing, lack of access to grocery stores and medical facilities, and resulting health disparities. These people of color are dying at higher rates than White people in part because the work they do has been deemed "essential," putting them at increased risk of infection. Indeed, they are the Walmart employees, the Instacart shoppers, the meatpackers, the migrant farmworkers, the grocery store clerks and the hospital workers who make it possible for the rest of the nation to work from home, order dinner in and watch Netflix. Rather than "essential," a more appropriate word might be "sacrificial." Furthermore, as the labor market deteriorates, they are among the first to be furloughed and laid off. A June 2020 report by the Economic Policy Institute found that women in general, but Black women more than any other group, have faced the largest losses. "'We're all in this together' has become a rallying cry during the coronavirus pandemic. While it is true that COVID-19 has affected everyone in some way, the magnitude and nature of the impact has been anything but universal," the report said. Less frequently discussed, but worthy of mention here given the focus of this text, is the fact that even those workers whose jobs can be done remotely do not necessarily have equal access to the technologies, space or time required to do so. Black and Latino workers are more likely than White workers to lack access to high-speed internet required for teleconferencing and more likely to live in multi-generational homes with less space and greater caregiving responsibilities.

As the pandemic rages on, millions of Americans have taken to the streets to protest killings of Black people. America has a long history of these killings, going all the way back to slavery, but a handful of cases in the past year have, at least it seems, put America on a course toward reckoning. A law enforcement officer fatally shot 28-year-old Atatiana Jefferson, a Black woman who worked in pharmaceutical equipment sales, through a window of her home in Texas in October 2019. A group of White men hit with a truck and then gunned down Ahmaud Arbery, a 25-year-old Black man who wanted to become an electrician, while he was taking a jog in Georgia in February 2020. Police killed 26-year-old Breonna Taylor, a Black emergency medical technician, while she was sleeping in her apartment in Kentucky in March 2020. The police killing of 46-year-old George Floyd, a Black man who lost his job as a bouncer in Minnesota during the coronavirus shutdown, was documented in May 2020 in a graphic video wherein he told officers "I can't breathe" and cried out for his dead mother. We include here these dead Americans' professions and professional dreams because it is important for White employers and workers to consider that their colleagues of color are not even safe in their own homes and neighborhoods. Venturing out to the office, to see a client or to a work site carries even greater risk.

The Lived Experience

The stories in this collection illuminate both the perniciousness of whiteness and the downright appalling manifestations of it in the workplace.

Most of the writers are people of color, who, as Lauren Michele Jackson of Northwestern University wrote in *Slate*, "are by default experts on racial interactions." A handful have been granted whiteness and explore how their whiteness has affected the trajectory of their careers, how it allows them to live their day-to-day work lives with less psychological harm, and how they have perpetuated whiteness at work. Some of the pieces describe overt discrimination and hateful acts experienced by the writers themselves. Others describe how whiteness affected colleagues, clients, students and friends.

In "You're Killing Me With Your Rhetoric: The Curious Case of the Angry Black Woman," forensic psychologist Stephanie Williams writes about being labeled an "angry Black woman" by a co-worker at a California jail and how daily oppression takes a toll on the bodies of people of color.

In "Not So Subtle: Whiteness Through the Eyes of an Immigrant of Color in the Academy," Jaime Antonio Rivera Flores offers a narrative of experiences and encounters with whiteness in academia. The chapter frames these stories within the historical context of whiteness studies in the United States. An immigrant from Mexico, the author concludes with a reflection about how personal narratives of this sort serve to complement theory, while making the conceptual more understandable and relatable.

In "Nine Sharp," satirist Dennard Dayle writes about going, as a fresh college grad, to a job interview at a New York fashion magazine, getting the position and looking for an escape hatch shortly thereafter.

In "Conquering Concord," lawyer Luisa Reyes tells a story about attending a Massachusetts chamber of commerce meeting with a Black colleague and learning after the fact that her experience was wildly different than her own.

In "The Monolingual Aspect of Whiteness at Work," Javier Sánchez reflects on the role of language in academia in relationship to the concept of whiteness. He critiques the persistent defense of English as the only viable medium for the transmission of intellectual knowledge by (usually) White, monolingual faculty members and administrators. Indeed, this outlook undermines and contradicts (often their own) efforts to globalize and internationalize the curriculum while preserving a traditional, patriarchal, White, Anglo-centric, colonial view in academia.

In "Safe Zone," the pseudonymous tano rubio recalls his experience as a first-year teacher in an alternative school. Centering on a conversation with a couple of students during a lockdown, he explores his own racial identity while trying to navigate and foster a safe space amidst a tumultuous academic environment for himself and other minorities.

In "Let's Talk About It: White Discrimination—an Act of Domestic Terrorism," Lucía Galleno Villafán writes about her encounters with discrimination by White people (what she terms "White discrimination") in the United States. She reflects on the (quickly dispelled) illusions of America that she held as a new immigrant; the cultural inferno that racism produces; and opportunities for new dialogues capable of eroding racism.

In "The Fight Against White Privilege," Mark E. Attucks Sr. writes about retiring from the military after 30 years of service, becoming an executive for megaretailer Target, and then returning to government service at the highest level. All the while, he had to fight tooth and nail for the recognition and compensation he deserved.

In "In Academia, the Gates of Entry and Advancement Are Guarded by Those Who Uphold White Supremacy," Michael A. Moreno writes about how engaging in anti-racist teaching practices made him a target for harassment and ultimately put his academic career in jeopardy.

In "Toward Restoration and Justice: Whiteness in Higher Education and Teaching Anti-Racism," public health graduate student Jacqueline Lantsman interrogates how her whiteness at the front of the classroom undermined her anti-racist course curriculum and argues that restorative justice practices in such settings could help de-center whiteness and elevate the voices of students of color.

Each story is true and has a lesson or lessons to teach us. In *Seeing White*, Halley et al. ask their readers: "If whiteness is normal, what does that communicate about the experience of other races?" We hope our book brings to life the answer to that question. We also hope it shows that no workplace is neutral. We all must play active roles in expelling whiteness from our workplaces.

Sources

Barroso, A.R. 2019. "The Wage Gap for Women of Color Widened in 2017." *National Women's Law Center*, January 29, 2019. nwlc.org/blog/the-wage-gap-for-women-of-color-widened-in-2017/.

Bash, D., & Nolan, B. 2019. "These Five Freshman Congresswomen Changed History by Becoming Unlikely Leaders on Impeachment." *CNN.com*, September 28, 2019. cnn.com/2019/09/28/politics/badass-women-impeachment-democrats-oped/index.html.

Bates, K.G. 2017. "New Evidence Shows There's Still Bias Against Black Natural Hair." *National Public Radio*, February 6, 2017. npr.org/sections/codeswitch/2017/02/06/512943035/new-evidence-shows-theres-still-bias-against-black-natural-hair.

Davidson, J. 2019. "Latest Federal Diversity Report from OPM Shows Little or No Progress and Some Regression." *Washington Post*, March 31, 2019. washingtonpost.com/news/powerpost/wp/2018/04/02/latest-federal-diversity-report-from-opm-shows-little-or-no-progress-and-some-regression/.

DiAngelo, R. 2011. "White Fragility." *International Journal of Critical Pedagogy*, 3(3). 54–70. libjournal.uncg.edu/ijcp/article/viewFile/249/116

Durr, M., & Wingfield, A.M.H. 2011. "Keep Your 'N' in Check: African American Women and the Interactive Effects of Etiquette and Emotional Labor." *Critical Sociology*, 37(5), 557–571. doi: 10.1177/0896920510380074

Evans, R.J. 2019. "From Nazism to Never Again." *Foreign Affairs*, August 26, 2019. foreignaffairs.com/articles/western-europe/2017-12-12/nazism-never-again.

Friedmann, J. 2009. "Dubious Role Models: Study Reveals Many German Schools Still Named After Nazis." *Spiegel Online International*, February 4, 2009. spiegel.de/international/germany/dubious-role-models-study-reveals-many-german-schools-still-named-after-nazis-a-605223.html.

Garcia, S.E. 2017. "The Woman Who Created #MeToo Long Before Hashtags." *New York Times*, October 20, 2017. nytimes.com/2017/10/20/us/me-too-movement-tarana-burke.html.

Gee, B., & Peck, D. 2018. "Asian Americans Are the Least Likely Group in the U.S. to Be Promoted to Management." *Harvard Business Review*, May 31, 2018. hbr.org/2018/05/asian-americans-are-the-least-likely-group-in-the-u-s-to-be-promoted-to-management.

Gerdeman, D. 2017. "Minorities Who 'Whiten' Job Resumes Get More Interviews." *Harvard Business School Working Knowledge*, May 17,

2017. hbswk.hbs.edu/item/minorities-who-whiten-job-resumes-get-more-interviews.

Gould, E., & Wilson, V. (2020) "Black workers face two of the most lethal preexisting conditions for coronavirus—racism and economic inequality." *Economic Policy Institute*, June 1, 2020. epi.org/publication/black-workers-covid/

Grieco, E. 2018. "Newsroom Employees Are Less Diverse Than U.S. Workers Overall." *Pew Research Center*, November 2, 2018. pewresearch.org/fact-tank/2018/11/02/newsroom-employees-are-less-diverse-than-u-s-workers-overall/.

Green, E. 2016. "Can Jews Still Assume They're White?" *The Atlantic*, December 8, 2016. theatlantic.com/politics/archive/2016/12/are-jews-white/509453/.

Hernandez, M., & Avery, D.R. 2016. "Getting the Short End of the Stick: Racial Bias in Salary Negotiations." *MIT Sloan Management Review*, June 15, 2016. sloanreview.mit.edu/article/getting-the-short-end-of-the-stick-racial-bias-in-salary-negotiations/.

Hilger, N. 2016. "Upward Mobility and Discrimination: The Case of Asian Americans." *National Bureau of Economic Research*, October 19, 2016. nber.org/papers/w22748.

Hispanic Association on Corporate Responsibility. 2016. "Corporate Inclusion Index." hacr.org/wp-content/uploads/2018/02/2016-HACR-CII.pdf.

Jackson, L.M. 2019. "'White Fragility' Has a Whiteness Problem." *Slate*, September 5, 2019. slate.com/human-interest/2019/09/white-fragility-robin-diangelo-workshop.html.

Jameel, M., & Yerardi, J. 2019. "Workplace Discrimination Is Illegal. But Our Data Shows It's Still a Huge Problem." *Vox*, February 28, 2019. vox.com/policy-and-politics/2019/2/28/18241973/workplace-discrimination-cpi-investigation-eeoc.

Johnson, A.M.G., Godsil, R.D., MacFarlane, J., Tropp, L. R., & Goff, P.A. 2017. "The 'Good Hair' Study Results." *Perception Institute*. perception.org/goodhair/results/.

Jones, S. 2017. "7 in 10 Senior Executives Are White Men." *Fortune*, June 10, 2017. fortune.com/2017/06/09/white-men-senior-executives-fortune-500-companies-diversity-data/.

Kohut, A. 2015. "Are Americans ready for Obama's 'Middle Class' Populism?" *Pew Research Center*, February 19, 2015. pewresearch.org/fact-tank/2015/02/19/are-americans-ready-for-obamas-middle-class-populism/.

Lee, C. 2017. "Here's How the Sound of Your Voice Can Hold You Back in Your Career." *Forbes*, January 5, 2017. forbes.com/sites/break-the-future/2016/12/28/heres-how-the-sound-of-your-voice-can-hold-you-back-in-your-career/.

Liu, E. 2014. "Why are Hispanics Identifying as White?" *CNN.com*, May 30, 2014. cnn.com/2014/05/29/opinion/liu-study-hispanics-favor-whiteness/index.html.

Mahdawi, A. 2017. "I'm a Bit Brown. But in America I'm White. Not for Much Longer." *The Guardian*, March 21, 2017. theguardian.com/commentisfree/2017/mar/21/us-census-whiteness-race-colour-middle-east-north-africa-america.

McElroy, K. 2019. "Why Don't Newsroom Diversity Initiatives Work? Blame Journalism Culture." *Poynter*, August 7, 2019. poynter.org/reporting-editing/2019/why-dont-newsroom-diversity-initiatives-work-blame-journalism-culture/.

Pager, D. 2003. "The Mark of a Criminal Record." *American Journal of Sociology*. doi.org: 10.1086/374403.

Painter, N.I. 2010. *The History of White People*. New York: W.W. Norton & Company.

Phillips, D.C. 2018. "Do Low-Wage Employers Discriminate Against Applicants with Long Commutes? Evidence from a Correspondence Experiment." *Journal of Human Resources*. doi: 10.3368/jhr.55.3.1016-8327r

Phillips, D. 2018. "Research: Hiring Managers Are Biased Against People with Longer Commutes." *Harvard Business Review*, December 10, 2018. hbr.org/2018/12/research-hiring-managers-are-biased-against-people-with-longer-commutes.

Quillian, L., Pager, D., Hexel, O., & Midtbøen, A.H. 2017. "Meta-analysis of Field Experiments Shows No Change in Racial Discrimination in Hiring Over Time." *Proceedings of the National Academy of Sciences*, 114(41), 10870–10875. doi: 10.1073/pnas.1706255114

Suarez, C. 2018. "The Nonprofit Racial Leadership Gap: Flipping the Lens." *Nonprofit Quarterly*, September 17, 2018. nonprofitquarterly.org/nonprofit-racial-leadership-gap-flipping-lens/.

Younis, M. 2019. "Most Americans See American Dream as Achievable." *Gallup*, September 4, 2019. news.gallup.com/poll/260741/americans-american-dream-achievable.aspx.

You're Killing Me with Your Rhetoric: The Curious Case of the Angry Black Woman

Stephanie N. Williams

It starts like another workday.

I am tired from the balancing act of being a working mother. I'm tired from living in a community where only 3 percent of the population looks like me. I'm tired from working in a jail system where I see Black and Brown bodies incarcerated at higher rates and for longer times than their White peers, and I am tired of paying more to have less.

But on this day, like many other days, I come into work and put on my best smile and demeanor, ready to fight the good fight.

I had decided to talk with a co-worker who had been making negative comments about my qualifications. I request the help of a neutral party to act as an observer, and then I sit down with my co-worker.

I am immediately bombarded with definitive statements:

"You're difficult, overly aggressive."

"You are hard to communicate with, aloof."

"Every time I talk with you, I feel like you're going to blow up at me, and I don't feel safe with you."

These words spin in my mind like a tornado, and I think to myself: *Stay composed, ask for examples, be clear and tempered in your tone, and offer to make it better*. Ultimately, I leave the conversation recognizing this unique feeling of humiliation that is directly related to being stereotyped as an angry Black woman.

***

I have been a mental health professional for 14 years. Like many women of color, my trajectory was filled with ups and downs. While in undergrad, I applied and was accepted to several terminal master's degree programs but no doctoral programs. At my college graduation, I was the topic of many conversations. "Oh, did you hear Stephanie is going to graduate school?" A professor who had written me letters of recommendation asked, "So, what are you going to do?" and they seemed truly surprised that I was, in fact, attending a graduate program.

After completing my master's in psychology, I applied to two doctoral programs. During one interview, I was asked why there was such a difference between my undergraduate GPA of 2.85 and my graduate GPA of 4.0. I explained the impact of poor academic funding in urban settings for students of color and how that significantly impacted my transition to college. My response was met with skepticism, and I was denied admission. During another interview, when I was asked if I thought I had the academic prowess to be successful, I decided to respond with a less direct answer: "I believe so." I was accepted.

After one semester, I decided to leave the school because of the blatant discrimination in the admission process, a lack of understanding of cultural sensitivity, and my poor personal adjustment to the cultural norms of Southern culture, being a native New Yorker. During this break from academia, I worked for five years as a licensed professional counselor in private practice, forensic settings, and nonprofits. I then applied to a progressive graduate program in California, where, after five years of clinical training, I received my doctoral degree. I have been employed as a forensic psychologist for the past five years.

As a forensic psychologist, I have firsthand knowledge of how biased the criminal justice system can be when it comes to people of color. Black males are about six times more likely to be incarcerated than their White peers; and, although Black Americans account for only 13 percent of the population, they account for 27 percent of arrests. Similarly, Black youth account for 15 percent of the U.S. population but make up some 35 percent of arrests (Sentencing Project 2018). Black women experience similar injustices. They are three times more likely than White women to be incarcerated (Kerby 2012; Sickmund, Sladky, Kang & Puzzanchera 2011).

As a Black person, I understand that 20 percent of the homes purchased by Black and Latino families are "higher priced," as defined by the government, compared with only 6 percent of homes purchased by White families and 4 percent of homes purchased by Asian families (Harney 2019). Research has also shown that there are large differences in the amount of credit offered to similarly qualified applicants in Black versus White communities (Cohen–Cole 2008) and that race affects the likelihood of a person obtaining a credit card, the number of credit cards they own, the credit line per card, and the conditions and fees attached to the card. These differences occur despite there being no difference in the rates of bad or good credit between Black and White households (Freeman 2017).

At the time of the incident I described at the start of this essay, I was on track to become promoted and was working very diligently to secure a seat at the table. I had the years of experience, both at the master's and doctoral levels; I had a strong vision for the department; and I already had implemented several key programs that shaped the county mental health system. While waiting for the opportunity to apply for advancement, I was told that a co-worker had been speaking negatively of my work ethic, abilities and qualifications to superiors for months, which prompted the intervention. I could not endure one more injustice outside my daily encounters with inequity.

***

When I approach my colleague, I am already fatigued from dealing with the daily demands of being Black in America. I am anxious about how to broach this difficult conversation, while understanding that I cannot swallow another injustice, especially one that is within my own control.

She is defensive and becomes more rigid in her body posture. I make sure to become more open and relaxed.

As she becomes loud and demanding, I remember to speak softly and calmly because I know the appearance of this situation is more important than the facts.

***

Like much of the negative imagery surrounding Black Americans, the stereotype of the "angry Black female" has its origins in 19th-century minstrel shows (Prasad 2018; FSU 2019). During this time, White actors wore blackface and portrayed the most extreme and negative stereotyped behavior representing Black women. The audiences had little to no real-life experience or interactions with Black women. These portrayals were an attempt to entertain the audience at the expense of Black women. These shows also were interpreted by the audience to be accurate representations of what to expect when dealing with Black women. For example, the "Sassy Mammy," which was later termed "Sapphire," shows Black women to be irrational, hostile, mean-spirited, and quick-tempered (Ashley 2014; Pilgrim 2008).

Even in the 21st century, the legacy of minstrel shows continues to perpetuate these false narratives of the stereotyped Black woman, through shows that display one-dimensional Black women as aggressive, feisty or loud (i.e. more dangerous) while simultaneously ensuring Black women conform to societal standards for racial- and gender-appropriate behavior (FSU 2019; Ashley 2014).

These negative stereotypes have real-world consequences for Black women when working, with Black women being held to higher standards, while simultaneously being assumed to be less qualified than their White peers and males (Washington & Roberts 2019). The continued prominence of this stereotype comes from being Black and exemplifying "nonconforming femininity" (Jones & Norwood 2017; Ashley 2014).

***

This is not my first time being labeled angry and likely won't be my last, so I understand this experience on two levels.

First, I recognize the seriousness of my colleague's accusation.

Second, I identify the immediate need to protect myself against any further damage to my professional reputation.

So, I develop a game plan:

How do I prevent this racist dog whistle from negatively influencing the opinions of my superiors?

How do I prove myself to be a level-headed, logical professional?

How can I protect my career?

And the most menacing thought: *How will this play out in the broader context of White femininity and White female victimhood?*

***

Black women historically have not been—and continue to not be—viewed as victims under any circumstances. During the women's suffrage movement, Sojourner Truth, giving a speech, asked the audience: "Ain't I a woman?" She noted that her (unique) position in the world was not one of "femininity" as defined by the male viewpoint of the time, but she was still a woman (NPS 2017). The societal ideal of normative femininity is a male-constructed paradigm where women are coerced to live up to expectations where their bodies, in both gesture and appearance, are visibly feminine. This unique construct is not race-neutral and, in fact, is formed under a strict lens of whiteness, leaving women of color the choice to either aspire to whiteness or be left out of the benefits afforded to women who are deemed feminine. The concept of femininity has been difficult for Black women because "they have historically been treated as though they exist outside of its boundaries" (Collins 2000). Qualitative studies show that Black women understand that normative femininity places them at a disadvantage, both in comparison to White women and in the eyes of men (Collins 2000).

During the fight for equal rights, Black women have been caught between civil liberties and feminism, creating the need for the understanding of intersectionality (Crenshaw 1989). Intersectionality states that Black women are routinely caught in the intersection of race and sex—causing Black women to experience a double discrimination because our experience of sexism is not deemed valid if White women are present and our experiences of racism are not deemed valid if there are Black men present.

The concept of White female victimhood is often explored under the lens of the Privilege Identity Exploration (PIE) model, which was coined by Sherry K. Watt (2007). While White women experience discrimination based on gender, they also experience the privilege afforded to them by their whiteness. The duality in identity that White women hold is a source of tension and/or blind spot when they are challenged by women of color to consider their privilege (Accapadi 2007).

White women have been depicted as the foundation of purity, virtue and beauty, and this privilege is bound to the image of powerlessness (Palmer 1994) or being the eternal victim. It is this state of powerlessness, which is shaped by historical context of what it means to be a woman in White society, that is an act of privileged femininity. This type of femininity is often wielded by White women in the form of tears—to secure their protected and often privileged place in femininity by ensuring others see them as victims. This act silences and harms women of color due to the discriminatory beliefs that women of color do not have the same level of femininity (i.e. powerlessness) as White women. Black women continue to be unprotected and voiceless in a world that prioritizes a man's strength (in a patriarchal society) and the perception of fragility (White femininity).

The complexity of bias that Black women face in the workplace is heightened by White fragility. The concept of White fragility suggests that Western society insulates and protects White people from truly addressing race-based stressors. As Robin DiAngelo explains, "Whites have not had to build the cognitive or affective skills or develop the stamina that would allow for constructive engagement across racial divides" (2011). It is this lack of awareness of the intolerance for racial stress that, when challenged, causes aggressive and/or passive-aggressive tactics in the workplace. These tactics single out the person of color as the instigator or the alleged problem needing to be fixed.

In the workplace, historical stereotypes of Black woman, White fragility and narrow concepts of femininity represent a trifecta of taxing experiences of constant hostility and oppression (Ashley 2014; Crenshaw 1989). It is this trifecta that positions me and other Black women in an arena where we are constantly misrepresented, misunderstood and almost certainly without the support of colleagues and superiors.

***

Black women working in systems that uphold systemic racism are mocked, met with unnecessary hesitancy, labeled and made to believe we are unworthy of the spaces we hold. These experiences occur while we are managing the demands of being professionals, wives, mothers, sisters, and daughters. Experiences like these take up space our minds and spirits, causing restless nights, wearing on the already depleted resources that we need to navigate the world, and deteriorating our overall health.

Studies show that Black women overwhelmingly participate in the workforce and have a desire to excel at their chosen careers, but their jobs are less stable than those of White women (Mays 2015). We are perceived as less capable and offered fewer opportunities while simultaneously carrying a heavier load than our White female counterparts (Mays 2015). To have the added daily pressure of dealing with stereotypes, racial bigotry and coded language, because we are uniquely feminine and discernably Black, is just plain exhausting.

The health consequences of racism, specifically for Black women, are well documented. Researchers have found a relationship between perceived racism and elevated blood pressure (Armstead, Herbert, Griffin & Prince 2014; Din–Dzetham, Nembhard, Collins & Davis 2004; Dolezsar, McGrath, Herzig & Miller 2014). Racism increases cortisol levels in people of color, and it has been suggested that long-term activation of stress responses can impact the flexibility of neural functioning affecting emotions, attention and other cognitive functions (Berger & Saynari 2014). Some researchers conclude that racism is a contributing factor to obesity (Cozier et al. 2009), anxiety (Maddox 2013), eating and other mental health disorders in Black women (Lacey et al. 2015; Mays 1995). Other health disparities found in the Black female community include alopecia (Thompson et al. 2018), poor cardiovascular health (Pool et al. 2017) and depression (Perry, Harp & Oser 2015; Lacey et al. 2015). Overall, discrimination related to sex and gender increases the risk of poor health and reduces well-being in Black women, ultimately making Black women more vulnerable to other complications that are associated with daily individual stress (Perry, Harp & Oser 2015).

***

Though I am frustrated and overwhelmed, because I understand these factors on a professional and personal level, after the confrontation with my co-worker, I set out to protect my career and myself.

I have no time to heal, no time to process, only time to act.

I use the privileges I have been afforded through education to jump into an all-too-familiar role that people of color endure daily: the role of being a racial ambassador.

I outline the historical and professional concerns of being labeled "angry" to the chair of the medical department.

I explain the contextual significance while also providing a very detailed explanation of the impact and discriminatory practices of covert racism and dog whistles in the workplace.

I explain the steps I took to protect myself against future reprisal: drafting a formal letter of concern, highlighting the neutral party who observed the interaction, and documenting my track record of professionalism.

I use this moment to teach the chair how these words impact people of color, why they impact people of color, and the importance of understanding bias in the workplace.

***

Ambassadorship suggests that people of marginalized groups should and can change the negative views of White privileged groups by "being beyond moral reproach" (Demby 2016). This added role requires the person of color to act selflessly by engaging in questions and entertaining the doubts of White people who have done little work when examining issues related to racism and privilege (Halloway 2015). This role requires one to methodically attempt to restructure, teach, and often entertain harmful ideology to help others think critically about issues related to race, class and privilege. This is a role that Black people are constantly asked to engage in without compensation, causing added fatigue and unnecessary stress (Halloway 2015).

***

While my efforts do not go unnoticed, they do seem to fall on deaf ears. Before I can request a formal investigation, the chair contacts me.

"I heard you were really rough with [said coworker]," the chair said.

I am caught off guard.

Although I seemingly did everything right, my co-worker's narrative prevailed, and I was deemed the aggressor. Despite my neutral party, despite my clear timeline of events and despite my explanation of how harmful this situation could be to my career, she was labeled the victim.

***

Ultimately, the ongoing battle to set clear boundaries and assert my humanity in a system that tries to dehumanize me daily is what whiteness in the workplace looks like.

To say this was a typical day in the life of a Black woman trying to navigate White professionalism would be an understatement. Without fail, I am asked to show up daily with the threat of being called angry. I am asked to perpetuate the status quo in order to maintain professionalism, all while experiencing dire health and emotional consequences because of it.

To quote Zora Neal Hurston: "If you are silent about your pain, they'll kill you and say you enjoyed it" (1937).

Sources

Accapadi, M.M. 2007. "When White Women Cry: How White Women's Tears Oppress Women of Color." *The College of Student Affairs Journal*, 26(2), 208–215.

Armstead, C.A., Hebert, J.R., Griffin, E.K., & Prince, G.M. 2014. "A question of color: The influence of skin color and stress on resting blood pressure and body mass among African American women." *Journal of Black Psychology*, 40:121–450.

Ashley, W. 2014. "The Angry Black Woman: The Impact of Pejorative Stereotypes on Psychotherapy with Black Women." *Social Work in Public Health*, 29(1), 27–34.

Berger, M., & Sarnyai, Z. 2015. "More Than Skin Deep: Stress, Neurobiology and Mental Health Consequences of Racial Discrimination." *Stress*, 18(1):1–10.

Cohen–Cole, E. 2011. "Credit Card Redlining." *Review of Economics and Statistics*, 93(2): 700–713.

Collins, P. H. 2000. *Black Feminist Thought* (2nd edition). New York: Routledge.

Cozier, Y.C., Wise, L.A., Palmer, J.R., & Rosenberg, L. 2009. "Perceived Racism in Relation to Weight Change in the Black Women's Health Study." *Annals of Epidemiology*, 19:379–387.

Crenshaw, K. 1989. "Demarginalizing the Intersection of Race and Sex: A Black Feminist Critique of Antidiscrimination Doctrine, Feminist Theory and Antiracist Politics." *University of Chicago Legal Forum*, 1989, 139–167.

Demby, G. 2016. "Who Should Do the Hard Work of Being the Race Ambassador?" *National Public Radio*, November 18, 2016. npr.org/sections/codeswitch/2016/11/18/502199116/who-should-do-the-hard-work-of-being-the-race-ambassador

DiAngelo, R. 2011. "White Fragility." *International Journal of Critical Pedagogy*, 3(3), 54–70.

Din–Dzietham R., Nembhard W.N., Collins, R., & Davis, S.K. 2004. "Perceived Stress Following Race-Based Discrimination at Work is Associated with Hypertension in African Americans. The Metro Atlanta Heart Disease Study, 1999–2001." *Social Science & Medicine*, 58:449–461.

Dolezsar, C.M., McGrath, J.J., Herzig, A.J.M., & Miller, S.B. 2014. "Perceived Racial Discrimination and Hypertension: A Comprehensive Systematic Review." *Health Psychology*, 33(1):20–34.

Freeman, A. 2017. "Racism in the Credit Card Industry." *North Carolina Law Review*, 95(4), 1071–1159.

Halloway, K. 2015. "Black People Are Not Here to Teach You: What So Many White Americans Just Can't Grasp." *Salon*, April 14, 2015. salon.com/2015/04/14/black_people_are_not_here_to_teach_you_what_so_many_white_americans_just_cant_grasp_partner/.

Harney, K. R. 2019. "Racial Disparities Significant in Mortgage Rejections, Study Shows." *Chicago Tribune*, May 20, 2019. chicagotribune.com/real-estate/ct-re-0527-kenneth-harney-20180521-story.html.

Hurston, Z.N. 1937. *Their Eyes Were Watching God*. New York: Harper Perennial.

Jones, T. & Norwood, K. 2017. "Aggressive Encounters & White Fragility: Deconstructing the Trope of the Angry Black Woman." *Iowa Law Review,* 102: 2017–2069.

Kerby, S. 2015. "The Top 10 Most Startling Facts About People of Color and Criminal Justice in the United States." *Center for American Progress*, May 29, 2015. americanprogress.org/issues/race/news/2012/03/13/11351/the-top-10-most-startling-facts-about-people-of-color-and-criminal-justice-in-the-united-states/.

Lacey, K.K., Parnell, R., Mouzon, D.M., Matusko, N., Head, D., Abelson, J.M., & Jackson, J.S. 2015. "The Mental Health of US Black Women: The Roles of Social Context and Severe Intimate Partner Violence." *BMJ Open*, 5.

Maddox, T. 2013. "Professional Women's Well-Being: The Role of Discrimination and Occupational Characteristics." *Women Health* 53, 706–729.

Mays, V. M. 1995. "Black Women, Work, Stress, and Perceived Discrimination: The Focused Support Group Model as an Intervention for Stress Reduction." *Cultural Diversity Mental Health*, 1: 53–65.

National Center for Juvenile Justice. (n.d.). "Easy Access to Juvenile Populations." Retrieved from ojjdp.gov/ojstatbb/ezapop.

National Park Service. 2017. "Sojourner Truth: Ain't I A Woman?" Retrieved from nps.gov/articles/sojourner-truth.htm.

Palmer, P.M. 1994. "White Women/Black Women: The Dualism of Female Identity and Experience." In *From Different Shores: Perspectives on Race and Ethnicity*, edited by R. Takaki, 167–174 (2nd ed.). New York: Oxford University Press.

Perry, B.L.; Harp, K.L.H.; & Oser, C.B. 2013. "Racial and Gender Discrimination in the Stress Process: Implications for African American Women's Health and Well-Being." *Sociological Perspectives*, 56(1): 25–48.

Pilgrim, D. 2008. "The Sapphire Caricature." Retrieved on August 28, 2019, from ferris.edu/HTMLS/news/jimcrow/antiblack/sapphire.htm.

Pool, L.R., Ning, H., Lloyd–Jones, D.M., & Allen, N.B. 2017. "Trends in Racial/Ethnic Disparities in Cardiovascular Health Among US Adults From 1999–2012." *Journal of the American Heart Association*, 6(9).

Prasad, R. 2018. "Serena Williams and the Trope of the 'Angry Black Woman'." *BBC*, September 11, 2018. bbc.com/news/world-us-canada-45476500.

Sickmund, M., Sladky, T.J., Kang, W., & Puzzanchera, C. 2011. *Easy Access to the Census of Juveniles in Residential Placement*. Retrieved from ojjdp.gov/ojstatbb/ezacjrp/.

The Sentencing Project. (n.d.). "Trends in U.S. Corrections." Retrieved from sentencingproject.org/publications/trends-in-u-s-corrections/.

Thompson, J.M., Park, M.K., Qureshi, A.A. (2018). "Race and Alopecia Areata Amongst US Women." *Journal of Investigative Dermatology Symposium Proceedings*, 19(1): 47–50.

Washington, Z., & Roberts, L. 2019. "Women of Color Get Less Support at Work. Here's How Managers Can Change That." *Harvard Business Review*, March 4, 2019. hbr.org/2019/03/women-of-color-get-less-support-at-work-heres-how-managers-can-change-that.

Watt, S.K. 2007. "Difficult Dialogues and Social Justice: Use of the Privileged Identity Exploration (PIE) Model in Student Affairs Practice." *College Student Affairs Journal*, 26(2), 114–126.

Not So Subtle: Whiteness Through the Eyes of an Immigrant of Color in the Academy

Jaime A. Rivera Flores

Attempting to discuss my experiences regarding whiteness in academia has proved to be a much harder task than I anticipated. I did not initially perceive the events described in this text as racialized encounters of oppression. That awareness only came to me years after some of them occurred. Furthermore, my first attempts at narrating them included personal comments of self-doubt and justifications about the individuals involved. Feedback from reviewers allowed me to distill the substance of each experience in order to provide a more succinct narration, but also to give each moment its proper importance: to validate the hurt that I felt and to see things for what they were, without the filter of trying to justify the microaggressors involved. Of course, my experiences in isolation cannot be understood without discussing first my vision on the state of the issues surrounding whiteness and how I see myself in relation to this topic. Therefore, I will begin by giving a broad panorama of whiteness studies. I will then proceed to narrate some of my encounters with whiteness in my work as an academic. In my conclusion, I explain that testimony like mine can help others have a more informed dialogue about issues of whiteness and how they affect all of us.

The history of whiteness is one of control and oppression. A first read of the concept may lead some to think that whiteness is a racial concept; however, the problem with whiteness begins precisely with the idea of race, since "[r]ace is a concept created in the modern era as a way of drawing distinctions between people such that some might benefit at the expense of others" (Nakkula & Toshalis, 2006, 123). Biologically speaking, race does not exist. Rather, as Milner pointed out, race is a concept built upon four basic constructs: 1) physical, "based on skin pigmentation," and refers to the fact that people, in fact, look differently around the world; 2) social, since societies have customs, traditions, and laws that create division between perceived races; 3) legal, because, throughout history, laws have referred to racial distinctions and inequalities; and 4) historical, due to the fact that it has been evident that people have treated each other differently over the years based on perceived racial differences (Milner 2015, 8–9). Whiteness, therefore, is only tangentially related to physical traits. Groups of people that today are deemed as unquestionably White were, just a century ago, subject to discrimination and oppression precisely for not being White. Indeed, "there was a time when the immigrants of New York City's Lower East Side—the Irish, Poles, Italians, and Russian and Eastern European Jews—were not considered white. But today, it appears they are" (Bergo & Nicholls, 2015, 7). One may be inclined to think that it is the light complexion of these groups that gained their entrance into whiteness. In fact, the passage from minority to mainstream has been a staggered process in which several different immigrant groups who arrived in the early 1900s gradually assimilated into the mainstream culture, adopted the English language, and now claim whiteness. In that fashion, Italian, Polish, and Irish immigrants, for example, are now considered White even though that was not the case in the early 1900s.

A clear start in whiteness studies in the United States can be traced back to 1936, with the publication of a book by William Edward Burghardt Du Bois, *Black Reconstruction in America 1860–1880*. Several authors credit Du Bois with starting a new wave of racial studies that have unveiled social evolutions, such as the ones described above, which clearly had their roots in cultural hegemony. "In *Black Reconstruction in America 1860–1880* (1936) Du Bois argued that white labourers in the United States came to embrace the racial identity of the dominant group, rather than adopt an identity framed around a class solidarity with recently freed slaves, because white workers received a 'public and psychological wage' by joining or at least queuing themselves up for admission into the white race" (Twine & Gallagher 2012, 4). In other words, from its inception, the idea of whiteness has been intertwined with mechanisms of control, domination, and economics in addition to social and psychological benefits. The elites decided to accept certain groups of workers who happened to have lighter complexions into the category of whiteness. Of course, this privilege perpetuated the oppression of darker-skinned individuals all whilst maintaining the existing hierarchy of social and economic strata. It must not have been difficult to convince these groups to accept the "White" label since "being defined by the courts as white granted rights to groups who were then able to lay claim to the resources (land, jobs, contracts, schools) that only whites could enjoy" (Twine & Gallagher, 2012, 8). This arrangement cemented the systemic inequality that perpetuated the discrimination against descendants of African slaves even if they belonged to the same economic class as other groups that had been recently elevated to whiteness. Marilyn Halter explained that "[e]arlier generations of ethnic Americans typically wanted to assimilate into the mainstream as rapidly as possible" (Halter 2000, 7). Their efforts to become White led them to stop speaking their native languages at home and to raise a generation of children who were unable to communicate with their grandparents. Although they lived in segregated communities, these immigrants attempted to *pass for White* and to become *more American* by adopting new behaviors even if they kept some of the traditions from their home countries. A fitting example of this transformation is that of the Jews. In Nazi Germany, Jews were discriminated against for not being White.[1] Propaganda exaggerated their physical features as ugly. Negative stereotypes were spread about them, many of which, sadly, persist. However, in the United States, Jews today are considered as White as any other Caucasian.

This process of whitening has been studied extensively. It has been in fact, one of the focal points of whiteness studies from its beginning, along with other important processes, such as the disenfranchisement of minority groups, to name just one. Twine and Gallagher identified what they called "waves" in whiteness studies, and the second wave they pinpoint in the production of these studies included "how racial minorities have been written out of history, the lack of attention to the way immigrants on the racial margins were whitened and the means by which culture and ideology work to constantly recloak whiteness as a normative identity" (Twine & Gallagher 2012, 8). The process of whitening a whole group of people is carried out within a society with such subtlety that most of the population is unable to perceive it. In fact, inconspicuousness might be a necessary element in this process, since those newly admitted as Whites will, obviously, not contest their newly gained benefits, and those who are still oppressed should not notice their continued abuse in light of the elevation of their former peers to a better social status. What the new Whites do not know, however, is that admittance into the construct of whiteness may only carry a psychological feeling of improvement without any other actual advantages associated to it. In the middle of those dynamics, "the invocation of white identities may suspend other social divisions and link people who share whiteness to dominant social locations, even though the actors are themselves in position of relative powerlessness" (Oluo 2018, 3). For example, the construct of the "White working class" includes mostly people

[1] In the late 1930s, Adolf Hitler sought to create a perfect society in Germany, and that included exterminating those individuals who did not fit the ideals he envisioned. Hitler considered the Aryan race as the ideal one. Since Jews were not Aryan, they were persecuted, and millions were killed during World War II.

who are towards the bottom of the socioeconomic ladder, but the fact that they are considered "White" makes them feel as if they are, in a hierarchical way, above others, that is, above people of color. This perception of superiority works as a hegemonic mechanism. White people who belong to the working class and/or other oppressed groups in society, such as the gay community, may even fail to perceive their situation of subjugation, in light of their White privilege, to the point that these individuals might advocate policies that affect them directly due to the fact that they choose their White identity marker above others that also apply.

When it comes to personal identity, several elements intersect to determine how each one of us is perceived. I believe I am perceived as a Mexican immigrant in the United States of America. What we call identity is not just one label, but a collection of constructs that influence one another in the context of a specific social group, or as Agius and Keep explain, "when we speak of 'identity' we are not simply classifying but, rather, engaging in a complex series of meanings, intersections and possibilities of being, and relating that construct to the fabric of social, political, cultural and economic life" (Agius & Keep 2018, 2). In that light, we cannot describe one label as an exclusive identity. At the same time, the combination of constructs that make up someone's identity may add or deduct value in an imaginary sum of someone's worthiness within a society. To the surprise of some, a label such as "man," which typically would be considered more valuable than the label "woman," when seen in a bigger context of intersections such as homosexual-black-Muslim-foreign-undocumented-man, ends up being placed much lower on the societal ladder than the intersection of heterosexual-White-Protestant-American-citizen-woman. The labels that comprise my identity are gay-Hispanic-(Mexican)-highly-educated-man, but that is just one part of the mix. One of the many elements in the construction of my identity is my phenotype or my physical appearance. I happen to have facial features that can be claimed by several different ethnicities. People from Egypt and India have asked me if I am native to their countries. Zeus Leonardo explains that "[b]eing racially ambiguous is a burden in a color-centered nation but it is also a gift, perhaps in Du Bois's sense, insofar as it exposes racial ambiguity and provides insight" (Leonardo 2009, 3). In my case, the burden is that I am immediately identified as foreign. My slight accent has sometimes led some people to assume that I do not speak English, especially if they ask me something and I take a little longer to answer than they expect. This fact was brought to the fore even more clearly to me when I married my husband, a light-skinned Mexican man. Even though he is less fluent in English than I am, people immediately assume that he is White and address him in English, whereas they look at me and speak Spanish. This happens before either of us utters a single word. At the same time, as Zeus Leonardo said, my light-brown skin and multiracial appearance has indeed allowed me to pay more attention to my own place in society, the way that I dress, and the facial features of people from the countries that claim similarity to my appearance.

The awareness of my being visibly not White in the context of the 21st century United States of America has also led me to be more vigilant about my interactions with authorities, since, as Middleton, Roediger and Shaffer, point out, "African Americans, Hispanics, and Indians in particular are frequently marginalized because they are not white. Furthermore, mixed-race individuals who may self-identify as 'white' are sometimes rejected by the majority for not being 'white' enough for acceptance under legal or community standards" (Middleton, Roediger & Shaffer 2016, 5). While I do not claim whiteness, I behave in ways that will not advertise my otherness too loudly. Still, I have seen examples of how I can be rejected within a community through subtle mechanisms. One of these instances is when I inquired at an apartment complex about the requirements to rent a unit. Good credit history was necessary. As a recent immigrant, I had no credit history in the United States yet. My parents' credit history from Mexico could not be used. I was not able to move into that apartment complex. Even though leasing companies may claim that asking for a credit report is a way to ensure that the new tenant will be responsible enough to pay for rent in the future, asking for a credit report eliminates all recent immigrants from the pool of applicants, even the ones with documented status. Asking for a paystub or proof of employment is another way of excluding certain groups like undocumented immigrants, who may receive their salary in cash. These excluded groups are "the others."

Being perceived as "the other" is an unavoidable consequence of having a darker complexion in the United States. Othering, as a verb, describes the action of treating people differently because of a perceived difference that excludes them from a group. Race is sometimes the one element that separates a social group from another. In that case, a set of racialization practices determines the treatment of different groups. As Carey, Boucher, and Ellinghaus put it, the "dynamics of racialization have often been maintained via the unbearable discursive weight of Othering" (Carey, Boucher & Ellinghaus 2009, 5). As discussed previously, every construction of identity, in one way or another, requires examining one's place in relation to a group, but also in contrast with other groups. This examination situates the individual in society. Amanda Lewis explained that "[h]ow people understand the world and their place in it necessarily affects how they operate and thus shapes the world in which they live" (Lewis 2004, 7).

Before coming to the United States, I had an identity that had to shift and adapt to the realities of the society where I lived. In Mexico I was part of the mainstream. Here in the United States, I had to learn that I was part of the Hispanic or Latino minority.

Being Hispanic or Latino in the United States is a relatively new concept. It is evident that "in the United States, the addition of the 'Hispanic' category to the 1970 census and the subsequent classification of individuals with Spanish surnames as 'Hispanic' or Latino has generated new identities and political constituencies at the federal and national level" (Twine & Gallagher 2012, 10). Interestingly enough, there are Hispanics of all races. There are White Hispanics as well as Black and Asian Hispanics, with all different shades of white, black, red and yellow. Yet precisely because there are Hispanics who can be perceived as White, the Hispanic category represents a challenge for racial hegemony. Philip Gleason pointed out that the category "white, not of Hispanic origin" has excluded Hispanics from being 100 percent White, but it has also excluded "European ethnic groups, who considered themselves minorities" from receiving minority benefits (Gleason 1992, 107). This is, of course, a two-sided instrument since government benefits are aimed at aiding those in need, and there are certainly White people in the lower strata of society who could benefit from government aid but who see themselves excluded from some programs due to the color of their skin. At the same time, separating Whites from Hispanics who see themselves as White—because they cannot possibly claim to be Asian, Black, Pacific Islander, Native American, nor do they feel that the other category applies to them—is a move that renders White Hispanics as inferior to Anglo-Saxon, Protestant Whites. That is how I feel when I face the demographics question of race. In the absence of a "Latino" or "Hispanic" race, which does not exist, I have to answer "White" because the other options do not apply to me: I am not Asian, nor Black, nor Pacific Islander, nor Native American. But I am obviously not the "pure" or "preferred" kind of White since I am invariably also asked either before or after the race question, whether I am Hispanic or Latino.

Further complicating the perception of my identity at the workplace is my legal status. Ever since I migrated to the United States, I have been fortunate enough to have held a visa—tourist, student, work—and now I hold a legal permanent resident card (green card). As a green card holder, I carry a Mexican passport, but I am a legal permanent resident of the United States. I have always been subject to taxation, although I did not always qualify for certain deductions from my paycheck, such as Social Security or Medicare. For the first five years, I paid taxes using the non-resident-alien tax forms. After five years in the country, all foreigners are mandated to file taxes as residents even if they are not residents for immigration purposes. Not being a citizen or a permanent resident always implied a series of restrictions. There was the time restriction: I was not able to stay in the U.S. indefinitely, just the duration of my visa, which was only one or two years, depending on the type of visa. The employment restriction: I was only able to work for the university where I studied or the employer who sponsored my work visa. There was also a mobility restriction: I was not able to travel freely. My visa could be denied when I applied for an extension, my entry into the country could be denied when I appeared at the port of entry (airport or border), and I could be deported at any time if there was a worthy reason for it. As a green card holder, I have the same rights as a citizen, except for voting or serving as a juror. I cannot vote in the United States, and I am not called for jury duty. I also cannot run for office until I become a citizen, and, even then, according to current laws, I will not be able to run for president, since I am not a "natural-born citizen." On the economic front, each time a visa is renewed, one must pay the filing fee whether the visa is approved or not. A United States visa fee is, at the time this text is being written, between $160 and $295, depending on the type of visa one is applying for. As a student, I had to renew my visa every two or four years, depending on the program of studies I was pursuing. As a work-visa holder, I applied for a visa every year. Each application involved returning to my home country and going to the embassy for a two-day process and waiting two weeks to one month for the visa to be mailed to me in Mexico. The American Embassy is not in the same city as my hometown, therefore I needed to travel to Mexico City for that two-day application process. Depending on where I attended graduate school or where I worked, round-trip plane tickets to go home cost between $550 and $900. Adding up the cost of the plane ticket, my stay in Mexico for about a month, and the visa application process, I had to budget for $1,000 to $1,500 every time I applied for a visa, which I did ten times in sixteen years, to keep my legal status in the United States. Maintaining legal status in this country is certainly a burden on the finances of certain individuals and their families.

The moment I received my green card, I had the freedom to work wherever I pleased. I was also granted the privilege of staying in the United States indefinitely. I did not depend on a visa renewal to stay in the country. But besides those external changes, I felt differently too. I was not afraid anymore of losing my legal status. I was not as worried anymore of having to go back to Mexico and find a job there after a decade and a half of living in the U.S. Before I held a green card, when I was on a student or work visa, if my sponsoring institution rescinded my visa, I had to go back to Mexico. As a green card holder, my legal status does not depend on my employment, and I could, if I needed to, look for a second job wherever I wished. In a few more years, I will be able to apply for naturalization to become a citizen of the United States, and it will be a transformative moment in my life. As Basler described it, "the naturalized individual, unlike the native-born citizen, must consciously engage the choice and process of joining the ranks of legitimate society. The acquisition of citizenship marks the beginning of full political and social membership in the US" (Basler 2012, 120). Once I become a citizen, the few limitations that I still face will disappear. I will be able to vote. I will be eligible to serve as a juror in court. I will be able to run for office and work at certain government agencies. Most importantly, this is something I have wanted for a long time. People sometimes ask why I have not become a citizen if I have been in the U.S. for so long. The answer is simple. There is no way to apply for citizenship without first being a permanent resident, and one does not become a permanent resident simply by asking to become one. Permanent residency can be obtained through employment, marriage/family sponsorship, investment (half a million dollars), and some other special circumstances. If one is not a millionaire, there is no I-want-to-become-a-permanent-resident form to be filled out to request a green card. But because I have sought to become a citizen of the United States for so long, I will cherish that citizenship when/if it is granted to me.

Ever since I moved to the United States, I have had several encounters that have underscored my not belonging to the White majority. This rejection from the majority group is quite remarkable to me because in Mexico I was part of the overwhelming majority of *mestizos*. And, even though skin color was a factor that determined one's place in society in Mexico, there I did not feel as an outsider, nor as a member of a minority, except for when it had to do with the category of sexual preferences, since I am a gay man. Having said that, I have lived in the United States for 19 years. I was 23 years old when I first arrived. By now, I have spent almost as much time here as I did in my home country.

As a graduate teaching assistant, and now as a university professor, I have had several experiences that have shown me the way whiteness works in the academic setting. My first observation was that, exactly like in Mexico, the group in the majority does not seem aware of the privileges that being in the majority afford them. White friends, co-workers, and students find it hard to acknowledge that they are in a position of advantage. This is because, as McIntosh points out, "there is a general resistance by white U.S. citizens to the idea that they have any unearned advantage and that systems of advantage exist" (McIntosh 2015, 17–18). Unless it is explained to them, many White individuals do not realize how lucky they are to be able to behave in certain ways that could be considered dangerous or reckless if their skin were darker. For example, one time at lunch, on campus, an older White male professor sitting at the same table as me, recounted a story of how he had been stopped by the police for a harmless infraction. When the police officer asked him how old he was, he joked and proceeded to give nonanswers. In sum, he did not treat the officer with respect because he thought the stop was not justified. From his account, the officer endured his jokes and let him go with a warning. When he finished giving his account, a White female professor sitting next to me and I looked at each other. I asked the older White male professor, "Do you know why you were able to joke like that with the police officer?" When my colleague suggested "Because I am older?" I said, "Well… yes, but also because you are a White male. If I had behaved that way, I would be in handcuffs or dead." He was not convinced that his being White had anything to do with how he had been treated.

In isolation, the behaviors discussed throughout these pages can be attributed to several reasons not related to whiteness. The people involved showed no malicious intent at the time of the event, and it would be easy to deny the fact that whiteness had a role in their actions. However, the danger in dismissing these actions as benign, and coming from good people, is that, as described by Cheryl Matias, "these 'not bad persons' need to realize how they are exerting whiteness regardless, and recognize the impact it has on people of color, fostering the institutionalism of racism and whiteness" (Matias 2016, 123). This is incredibly difficult. One does not always have the knowledge of why some actions are wrong; they just feel wrong. The setting at the time may not be conducive to a productive conversation. The tone used when confronting well-intentioned people must be watched carefully so as not to turn a good and professional relationship into a soured one. And, as explained by Cabrera, Franklin and Watson, "in ostensibly white environments, the normative pressure can push the targets of microaggressions to think that either they are reading too much into a 'nonracial' situation or they are being overly sensitive in the face of a microaggression (i.e. 'Am I going crazy?')" (Cabrera, Franklin & Watson 2017, 36). This is because these microaggressions are so subtle that the person at the receiving end of it may indeed question whether they are overreacting to an innocuous episode of daily life in the United States. After all, these behaviors are observed all around us, every day.

Even after years of living in the United States, I still find myself puzzled by new and unexpected behaviors from co-workers and students alike. I tend to believe in the maxim that states that the newer generations hold the future in their hands, and I see that with optimism. One cannot deny the progress that has been made in so many fronts when it comes to accepting social differences that just decades ago were considered taboo. Interracial marriage is now mostly a nonissue. Gay marriage is now the law of the land, and if, for some reason I must say in class that I am gay, no negative reaction has been observed for years, when loud gasps could be heard just ten years ago. However, as of late, the topic of White disenfranchisement has come to the fore in the classroom. Feagin explains that "while young whites are often portrayed in the mass media as liberal on racial matters, indeed much more so than parents and grandparents, in fact as a group they are racially illiberal" (Feagin 2005, xi). I was able to confirm this when a couple of semesters ago I taught a general education course at the institution of higher education where I work. Throughout that course, students are assigned several readings that allow them to learn their place in the universe with the objective of finding a sense of purpose in life. At the end of the course, we read Dr. Martin Luther King Jr.'s speech at the March on Washington. In the previous years of teaching, that speech inspired students to self-reflect on the progress that has been made in terms of civil rights, as well as the recent losses and the distance we still need to travel going forward. The conversations had always been enriching and enlightening. Yet, the last time, there was some reticence, and even hostility, from a couple of White male students. They were unwilling to recognize that further progress is necessary, not because people of color are finally treated equally, but because they saw the efforts to level the playing field as acts that were eroding their own rights instead of giving equal rights to others. It was even suggested that segregation was no longer the norm in this country. One of them went as far as to say that he even perceived reverse racism. Feagin confirms this perception: "Young whites feel that *they* now are the *victims* of reverse discrimination and affirmative action, or as now having a socioeconomic disadvantage in the United States" (Feagin 2005, xiv). This is a perfectly logical reaction to a more just reality. When a portion of the population has been treated with privilege for hundreds of years, it must be surprising for them to not receive those privileges anymore, or to see others receiving the same benefits that were originally afforded to only them.

In order to redirect the conversation, I mentioned that the U.S. population tends to divide racially every week at places of worship. I explained how that separation, even if it is not mandated, is segregation. The conversation became uncomfortable instead of inspiring. This experience helped me realize how complicated it is to approach these topics, which, even if addressed with the best of intentions, can become a point of contention and a reason to argue. In the literature about whiteness, some even suggest to not talk about whiteness. Linda Martín Alcoff explained that "the racial identity we call whiteness has been especially disavowed by some quarters of the white left on the grounds that it is a political construct that does nothing more than cloak the plutocracy. We should be tearing away the cloak, they argue, not giving into the idea that whiteness is real" (Alcoff 2016, 7). However, in order to tear the cloak away one must first recognize that there is a cloak to be torn away. More importantly, one must talk about one's own experience with regard to that cloak, especially if the one speaking is a person of color, since White voices have been heard for centuries. The discomfort that may be experienced while addressing these issues is a clear symptom of the dire need to resolve them. Or as Ijeoma Oluo puts it, "We have to be able to look racism in the eye wherever we encounter it…running won't help when it's in our workplace, our government, our homes, and ourselves" (Oluo 2018, 7). Regardless of how uncomfortable it may feel to bring up the subject, how open the racial wound still is, if we do not confront White privilege at the time and place where it is experienced, we are becoming a part of the problem because we are giving a tacit permission to others to continue to act in ways that infringe on our rights and that suppress our liberties. In the following pages, I will provide further examples of my encounters with whiteness in the workplace, because, as Mazurett–Boyle and Antrop–González stated, "our personal narratives aim to recognize our experiences not as tales of the marginalized but, instead, as valuable social and cultural capital resources others can use towards ending racism" (Mazurett–Boyle & Antrop–González 2013, 108). Telling our stories is not an exercise in self-pity; it is an exercise that documents the current state of affairs. It is this collection of stories that allows us to see ourselves in the mirror, and to show others how certain behaviors affect disenfranchised populations. When enough of these stories are collected, they become a body of evidence that supports the theoretical arguments brought up by scholars.

One of the many privileges that the White majority enjoys, without holding much regard for it, is "freedom of movement" (DiAngelo 2016, 178). Freedom of movement refers to being able to travel without hurdles or with minimal requirements. Undocumented immigrants in the United States often describe how helpless they feel about traveling long distances within the country. This is so because they fear being spotted as undocumented while going through the security line at the airport. Consequently, many undocumented individuals choose not to fly, even within the United States. I have never felt so restricted in my movement. However, as an immigrant, I do have extra hurdles when it comes to traveling in and out of the United States. Not only do I need to get in a different line at the airport, but I must have additional documentation that is not required of citizens. I must also be able to answer questions that are not asked of citizens. Depending on the type of visa, when an immigrant enters the United States, they must describe what they do for a living, what they intend to do in the U.S., for how long they intend to stay, and sometimes they must show documentation proving their claims. A further hurdle that restricts movement is not being able to renew certain types of visas from within the United States. Someone holding a student or work visa, as I once did, must go to the U.S. Embassy in their home country to get the newest stamp of approval in their passport. This paperwork cannot be completed in the United States.

In the summer of 2013, I was invited to take a group of students on a study-abroad trip to Spain. Because at the time I held a work visa that needed to be renewed every year, if I participated in that study-abroad trip, on my way back to the United States, I was going to have to travel to Mexico before coming back to the U.S. in order to get a visa renewal stamp on my passport. This extra stop in my trip meant additional expenses that the institution I worked for needed to incur if they sent me, as opposed to sending another professor who was a citizen. This extra requirement could have meant that someone else could have been chosen to lead the trip instead of me in order to save the institution money and/or time. After explaining the situation to the people in charge of logistics at the institution where I worked, my trip was approved. However, it became evident that I was not as free to travel as I pleased. Furthermore, even though my trip was approved, if I had been an American citizen, there would not have been any doubt that I could go on the trip. My trip had to be approved because of my extra requirements as a foreigner.

This lack of freedom when it comes to traveling abroad can be exacerbated if it is accompanied by microaggressions. Angelina Castagno points out that "within a frame of niceness, oppressive actions are not actually oppressive; they are just hurtful" but they do not stop being oppressive. In fact, she adds "whiteness thrives when we limit our understanding of inequity and dominance to individual intentions, knowledge, instances, and interactions" (10). In other words, when we dismiss some acts of aggression based on the perceived good intention of the person in question, we are legitimizing the interaction and allowing these acts to continue unchecked. While at my current institution, I wanted to continue to take students abroad. I led one trip while still holding a work visa, but when I was in the process of getting my green card, I spoke with the individual in charge of study abroad trips about my wanting to wait until my green card paperwork was finished before I submitted my application for my next trip. It simply was much easier for everyone if I traveled as a permanent resident instead of as a work-visa holder. That was my decision. When I had my green card in hand, I contacted the office in charge of trips letting them know that I was ready to submit my application for the next trip because I had finally received my green card. While discussing the trip with the person in charge, a few weeks before departure, I was asked, with what seemed like fake curiosity, what a green card looked like. I described it. She insisted that she wanted to see mine. I said that I did not carry it with me, but I could show her a photo. She agreed, but I could not locate the picture on my phone. I showed her a similar one from the internet. She insisted that she wanted to see *my* green card. I realized that she wanted to verify that I actually had a green card before she would let me travel. She did not say that explicitly, but I see no other explanation for that interaction. I scanned my green card at home and sent it to her. I did not want to think longer about what had happened. I just wanted to get that over with. The fact that this person was being nice to me while asking me for my papers did not make it any better. I did not understand at the time what part of the interaction made me so uncomfortable. After thinking about it, now I see that I have grown accustomed to a culture of trust in the United States. When someone is trustworthy, their word is taken at face value. At certain positions of power, one does not need to provide documentation for every claim one makes. As a professor, I had enjoyed that privilege. I had informed the office that I had a green card; my assumption was that they would believe that I had it. When I was asked to produce the evidence, I felt disrespected, especially because the request was disguised as pure curiosity. Perhaps if I had been told that they were checking all traveling documents for every participant in all trips, and that included passports, visas, green cards, and so forth, I would have produced my documents without hesitation. It was the sneakiness of the request that caught me off guard.

Other microaggressions have occurred when I have gone to the school cafeteria to have lunch. According to DiAngelo, front and backstage racism include "acting overly nice" or "mimicking" mannerisms (DiAngelo 2016, 141). A colleague who is now retired used to say hi to me in Spanish every time he saw me at lunch. He spoke to me in his broken Spanish in an exaggerated attempt to be cordial. His reactions sometimes included the words "ay ay ay." I tried to not find it offensive and justified him because he was an older White man who probably did not know better, but those were textbook microaggressions.

In my 19 years in the U.S., often at work, people ask me to represent "my people." DiAngelo says about nonwhites who are perceived as representatives of their race, that "whites may constantly ask them questions related to race, make racial jokes or comments they don't normally make with white people, ask personal questions about their racial experiences, ask them to speak on behalf of their group" (DiAngelo 2016, 225–226). When the Office of Admissions at my current institution wanted to organize a dinner for Hispanic prospective students, I was asked to give my input about the menu. The food that was going to be served was stereotypically Hispanic food. On the one hand, by being asked about this, I was able to steer them away from serving that food and probably offending potential students who would enroll at our institution. However, this instance showed me the lack of awareness of how some well-meaning actions could be interpreted by individuals who are constantly perceived as others.

This otherness is evident when meeting new people. While I was a graduate student in Florida, I tutored students during my free time. There was a list of approved tutors on the university website. People contacted me from seeing my name on that list. I remember a White woman who was a returning student in her late fifties or early sixties. We had been in touch through email. The first time we met, we arranged to go to the teaching assistants' office, in the language building on campus. It was probably 7 p.m. on a weekend. It was dark outside. The hallways did not have an automatic switch to turn on the lights, but some offices had the lights on. Since it was a little dark, as I approached her, she seemed afraid. In her mind, there was a man approaching her when she was expecting a woman. She later said that, based on my name (Jaime), she thought I was a woman. Her fearful reaction of just a few seconds had a lasting impact on me. I had never experienced something like that. I had never seen myself as a menacing figure. I immediately thought of how Black males tend to be perceived that way all the time, and, although that does not happen to me often, I had to learn to pay more attention to the way others perceive me because being unaware of how others see me could potentially put me in danger. As a result of this experience, if I am ever pulled over by a police officer for a traffic violation, I have become very aware of the fact that I need to be especially careful in the tone I use to talk to them and the speed of my movements because, unlike a White person, I am immediately perceived as a threat just due to the color of my skin.

This game of preconceived expectations happens often. When one morning I had to call security because the classroom where I was supposed to teach at my current institution was locked, the security guard—a young White woman—came to open the door, but before doing so, she asked who the professor was. I said it was me. She asked me for my ID. I produced it. She opened the door and left. However, I was feeling disturbed. I am sure that had I been an older White male, I would not have been asked to verify my claim that I was the professor. A combination of two factors—my being Hispanic and my looking somewhat young (I was 39 at the time, but I have been told that I look sometimes up to 10 years younger)—probably led the security guard to doubt my claim and check my credentials. I must say that I was dressed in formal clothes. No student dresses that way unless they have a job interview. While discussing the event with a White colleague, he told me that I should have felt flattered. I should have taken the security guard's actions as a compliment. I cannot do that. Of all the people waiting for the door to be open, it was me who greeted the guard. I thanked her for coming. I did look older than the average student. I was clearly overdressed to be a student. The most logical conclusion would have been that I was in charge. Therefore, I was the professor. Furthermore, there was no need for verification that a professor was around because it was regular business hours. Classrooms should not be locked at that time. Security could easily check that the room was booked for a class. The presence of a professor was not necessary to fulfill the request to unlock a room that should have been unlocked in the first place. Therefore, I believe it was my physical appearance that led the security guard to verify my identity. I felt discriminated against. I felt oppressed.

When microaggressions based on racial oppression are experienced everyday throughout one's life, it becomes a part of us, and it leads us to question our self-worth. DiAngelo states that "internalized racial oppression includes feelings of: self-doubt, inferiority, self-hate, powerlessness, hopelessness, apathy, generalized fear/anxiety" (DiAngelo 2016, 153–154). In other words, when one faces discrimination frequently, the accumulation of negative experiences leads one to believe there may be some truth to those negative views that others express about us. I have most often experienced those feelings of self-doubt, inferiority, powerlessness, apathy, and generalized anxiety when it comes to scholarship. The process of writing papers and getting feedback from colleagues has been frustrating. Getting a paper published involves receiving several rejections. For a White person, whose intelligence is not questioned every day, perhaps receiving constructive criticism may be plainly useful. However, for a member of a minority, criticism of almost any kind can have an enormous impact on one's ego to the point that it has led me to question whether I even deserve to be in academia. It is quite common for members of minority groups to experience impostor syndrome, which refers to the feeling of not being knowledgeable enough to be performing the tasks or doing the work one does, when, in reality, one is obviously qualified for the job. On the other hand, when others believe that a member of a minority is not capable of performing at the same level as a regular person based only on the fact that they belong to a minority, we are talking about "presumed mediocrity." I have been perceived to be incapable of certain actions due to my being

Hispanic several times. For example, despite the fact that I have lived in the United States for 19 years, completed two master's degrees and a Ph.D., in addition to having written my doctoral dissertation in English, there is a colleague who compliments my English when I use certain figures of speech. Comments like "great use of that expression" carry a good intention but are felt as microaggressions. They demonstrate my perception that this colleague has of me; that I don't speak English well. Whereas other people have praised my use of the English language, my "vast vocabulary," and the fact that I seldom make grammatical mistakes, this colleague seems surprised by the fact that I am able to use a fairly common idiom.

All of these experiences show me that whiteness, and the privilege and oppression that it extends to certain groups, continues to permeate the United States. It pervades all areas of academia, from the hallways of campus, and the cafeteria to the classrooms and across the institution as a whole. The importance of giving testimony is, first of all, to bear witness. At the same time, this unveiling of regular, typical interactions in the workplace as racialized events serves to open the eyes of individuals who may believe that we live in a post-racial society, or a colorblind society. As Lee Baker explained, "ideas about a color-blind society… erode the hard-fought victories of the Civil Rights Movement" (Baker 2001, 103) because they do not allow others to see that, in fact, we have not achieved racial equality. These testimonies also allow students and colleagues to have conversations in which they can reflect about the ways in which they may be perpetuating the injustices that whiteness harbors. By becoming aware of White underpinnings that pervade so many seemingly innocent interactions in our everyday lives, we can have a more informed dialogue about how to approach each other more mindfully. The awareness that arises from these dialogues can alert us about the ways that we replicate models of oppression to eradicate them in ourselves. At the same time, these conversations can help others to identify the same blind spots that once plagued us. It is through an individual effort of actively engaging in improving our relationships with others that we can make a difference, but it must start with awareness. Here is my testimony and, with it, my commitment to being more mindful in the classroom and, in general, in my interactions with students and colleagues, so as not to replicate, be it accidentally or unconsciously, mechanisms of White privilege.

Sources

Agius, C., & Keep, D. 2018. "The Politics of Identity: Making and Disrupting Identity." *The Politics of Identity: Place, Space and Discourse*, edited by Christine Agius and Dean Keep, 1–14. Manchester: Manchester University Press.

Alcoff, L.M. 2016. *The Future of Whiteness*. Malden, Massachusetts: Polity Press.

Baker, L.D. 2001. "The Color-Blind Bind." In *Cultural Diversity in the United States*, edited by Ida Susser and Thomas C. Patterson, 103–119. Malden, Massachusetts: Blackwell Publishers.

Basler, C. 2012. "White Dreams and Red Votes: Mexican Americans and the Lure of Inclusion in the Republican Party." In *The Future of Whiteness: A Map of the "Third Wave*," edited by Charles A. Gallagher & France Winddance Twine. New York: Routledge.

Bergo, B., & Nicholls, T. 2015. "Introduction: A Focus on White Privilege Through Personal Narratives." *I Don't See Color: Personal and Critical Perspectives on White Privilege*, edited by Bettina Bergo and Tracey Nicholls. University Park, Pennsylvania: The Pennsylvania State University Press.

Cabrera, N.L., Franklin, J.D., & Watson, J. 2017. *Whiteness in Higher Education: The Invisible Missing Link in Diversity and Racial Analyses*. Malden, Massachusetts: Wiley.

Carey, J., Boucher, L., & Ellinghaus, K. 2009. *Re-Orienting Whiteness: A New Agenda for the Field*, edited by Jane Carey, Leigh Boucher & Katherine Ellinghaus. New York: Palgrave McMillan.

Castagno, A.E. 2014. *Educated in Whiteness: Good Intentions and Diversity in Schools*. Minneapolis: University of Minnesota Press.

DiAngelo, R. 2016. *What Does It Mean to Be White? Developing White Racial Literacy*. Revised Edition. New York: Peter Lang.

Feagin, J.R. 2005. "Foreword." In *Being White*, by Karyn D. McKinney, xi–xv. New York: Routledge.

Garner, S. 2007. *Whiteness: An Introduction*. New York: Routledge.

Gleason, P. 1992. *Speaking of Diversity: Language and Ethnicity in Twentieth-Century America*. Baltimore: The Johns Hopkins University Press.

Halter, M. 2000. *Shopping for Identity: The Marketing of Ethnicity*. New York: Random House.

Leonardo, Z. 2009. *Race, Whiteness, and Education*. New York: Routledge.

Lewis, A.E. 2004. *Race in the Schoolyard: Negotiating the Color Line in Classrooms and Communities*. New Brunswick, New Jersey: Rutgers University Press.

Matias, C.E. 2016. *Feeling White*. Rotterdam, The Netherlands: Sense Publishers.

Mazurett–Boyle, R., & Antrop–González, R. 2013. "Our Journeys as Latin@ Educators and the Perpetual Struggle to Unhook from Whiteness." *Unhooking from Whiteness*, edited by Nicholas D. Hartlep and Cleveland Hayes, 103–122. Rotterdam, The Netherlands: Sense Publishers.

McIntosh, P. 2015. "Deprivileging Philosophy." In *I Don't See Color: Personal and Critical Perspectives on White Privilege*, edited by Bettina Bergo & Tracey Nicholls, 13–24. University Park, Pennsylvania: The Pennsylvania State University Press.

Middleton, S., Roediger, D.R., & Shaffer, D.M, eds. 2016. *The Construction of Whiteness: An Interdisciplinary Analysis of Race Formation and the Meaning of White Identity*. Jackson, Mississippi: University Press of Mississippi.

Milner IV, H.R. 2015. *Rac(e)ing to Class: Confronting Poverty and Race in Schools and Classrooms*. Cambridge, Massachusetts: Harvard Education Press.

Nakkula, M.J. & Toshalis, E. 2006. *Understanding Youth: Adolescent Development for Educators*. Cambridge, Massachusetts: Harvard Education Press.

Oluo, I. 2018. *So You Want to Talk About Race*. New York: Seal Press.

Twine, F.W. & Gallagher, C.A. 2012. "Introduction." In *The Future of Whiteness: A Map of the "Third Wave,"* edited by France Winddance Twine & Charles A. Gallagher. New York: Routledge.

Nine Sharp

Dennard Dayle

I like to think of myself as an original, or at least not a cliché. Sadly, we rarely live up to our self-image, and it's impossible for me to talk about my own experience without at least *nodding* at Lauren Weisberger. [1] Here's my abridged fashion intern experience, with less Prada and more spray tan. Names have been changed at my lawyer's desperate request.

My closet had thirteen superhero graphic tees, ten button-ups picked out by my mother, and a pair of sweaters I bought because I thought they "looked *Matrix*-y." [2] I should have read a call back from a fashion magazine as a dire omen and fled to the nearest church. Sadly, a few choice comments had me informally banned from every house of worship in Rutherford, New Jersey.

Maybe that attitude got me the call. Iconoclasm is always in vogue. Every medium appreciates subversion, and my habit of speaking without considering the immediate and obvious consequences is often mistaken for a genuine rebellious streak. As you'll soon learn, I'm much more comfortable sniping a few years after the fact.

That said, a fake rebel fit a magazine aimed at fake bohemians. *Nameless* wasn't found in the bathrooms of design movers, runway shakers, or even Anna Wintour's eyebrow brushers. It hid on the nightstands of quietly suicidal wine-bar partisans eternally "thinking of putting a portfolio together." An audience haunted by memories of cool, grasping at impressions of a time they understood the random whims of the zeitgeist. Instead of following one of the countless fully staffed daily, weekly, or monthly publications dedicated to cataloguing our cultural Alzheimer's,

---

[1] **Lauren Weisenberg:** The author of *The Devil Wears Prada*, a novel about an intern working for a cynical fashion icon that received a blockbuster Hollywood adaptation. Creative work I can now relate to far too closely.

[2] ***The Matrix*:** A seminal sci-fi action film that extrapolates Plato's "Allegory of the Cave" to people torrenting the ability to do Wuxia kung-fu. An ill-advised sequel is on the horizon.

they turned to a quarterly magazine about last year's media trends. This is the hipster version of hell.

I didn't have any of this healthy perspective when I took the call. All I knew was that it was a fashion magazine, an opportunity just cool enough to make my ex-girlfriend jealous. *Editorial intern* also sounded better than *unemployed*. As a graduate at the tail end of the recession, I was already tired of participating in June 2013's 7.5 percent unemployment rate.[3] I was doubly tired of the Black unemployment rate of 13.7 percent, which made me question the alternatives opened by my degree in "liking books." Chasing your dreams is more for some people than others.

"This is Anne, Pandora's personal assistant at *Nameless*. Could you come in at noon tomorrow to tell us a bit more about yourself?" Anne's voice sounded like a drowsy default answering machine.

"Sure."

"Actually, could you do 1:00?"

"Yes."

"Great, I'll pencil you in for 3:00."

An email came in asking me to come at 9:00. This was a dark and foreboding time of day for a recent graduate. The world before noon was mostly theoretical. I'd heard rumors of commuter trains and coffee carts, but I wasn't the superstitious type.

Despite NJ Transit, I reached Tribeca ten minutes early. Before knocking, I took a moment to clear my mind of expectations. Fashion was a scapegoat for the vapidity found in every branch of American culture. I'd seen bleach blondes holding small dogs lambasted in films, novels, comic books, music, and Tijuana bibles.[4] To succeed, I needed to forget the stereotypes and open my mind.

A bleach blonde clutching a tiny dog opened the door. She took off a pair of white-framed sunglasses to glare down at me. I could feel the scorn behind the Botox.

"When I say 9:00, I don't mean 8:55 or 8:57. I mean 9:00. Go get a coffee."

The door slammed shut. I marked the interview down as a loss, walked a lap around the block, and returned at 9:00 out of obligation. This time, I was greeted by a girl my age.

---

[3] "Bureau of Labor Statistics Data." U.S. Bureau of Labor Statistics, data.bls.gov/timeseries/LNS14000006.

[4] **Tijuana bibles:** Popular books of palm-sized, hand-drawn erotica printed in the United States during the Depression. The stereotypes leading to a U.S. production being called a Tijuana bible are likely the subject of another entry in this collection.

"You're Bernard, right? Follow me, Pandora will be with you in a minute." Judging by the voice, this was Anne. She looked more tired than she sounded.

"Dennard," I corrected as we walked.

"You'll love it here Ber…Den…dude. We've got a coffee machine, and you get to meet all kinds of famous people, and everyone knows each other's names."

I nodded dutifully, while trying to decide if the place could possibly be real. I associated "home office" with a startup owner's living room. At another internship, I'd spent one month pretending to work from the owner's kitchen. Emulating *Fire Emblem* (and half-assing one press release a week) to the hum of the fridge had been odd.[5] This was a different beast.

Movies occasionally set a scene in a pure white, harshly lit room. This usually marks some brush with the afterlife, or the point where *The Matrix* franchise completely collapsed. I never saw this in reality until I entered *Nameless*'s office. White chairs before white desks with white Apple desktops used by White people. Anne gestured to a white couch, and my paranoia kicked in. I imagined leaving a trail of inky black footprints made of every diseased puddle the Manhattan sidewalks had to offer.

The demographics were, in Pandora's defense, better than the national trend in some ways. United States newsrooms are whiter and maler than the nation at large. To be precise (in case you're the type that asks for more information before reaching for a pitchfork), Pew Research Center analysis says that U.S. newsrooms are 77 percent non-Hispanic White and 61 percent male.[6] So, while *Nameless* beat the curve on gender balance, they weren't winning awards on the racial front. Which explains where things went next.

Pandora returned with her dog at her heels. It sniffed me twice, decided I wasn't a threat to its status as alpha accessory, and ran off to bark at the art director. Pandora smiled as the art director shrank away from a creature the size of a football, and then took the seat opposite me. I imagined kicking a furry field goal as she pulled up my application.

Pandora traced my résumé with her finger as she read. The finger ran past my education and experience, settling on the "Service and Leadership" section.

"Leonard, you ran a dance company?" she asked.

---

[5] ***Fire Emblem***: A strategy/role-playing game franchise. Noted for featuring permanent character death, presumably to teach children about loss.

[6] Grieco, E. 2018. "Newsroom Employees Are Less Diverse Than U.S. Workers Overall." Pew Research Center, November 2, 2018. pewresearch.org/fact-tank/2018/11/02/newsroom-employees-are-less-diverse-than-u-s-workers-overall/.

"Dennard," I corrected. Tactical mistake. Pandora looked at me like I was wrong. "Err, yeah. In college."

"Princeton has break-dancers?" she asked, incredulous.

I nodded. My reaction during freshman orientation was similar. Princeton was designed for the stodgy villain bulldozing young dancers' community centers. Those alumni actually donated.

"Can you prove it?"

"Yeah, I have a few references."

"People can fake those. Can you dance for us here? Hiring honest people is very important to me."

iTunes replaced my résumé on her tablet. Two taps later, K.R.S.-One's "Sound of da Police" started playing from the overhead speakers.[7] This was, evidently, what middle-aged suburban refugees thought people bboyed to in 2015.[8] The rest of the office peered over and around their computers. This moment had been discussed.

When it feels like local reality is coming apart like a paper crane in a windstorm, I poke my tongue through one of my wisdom tooth gaps. Failing to find a cyanide tooth convinces me that I have to cope with the situation. In the *Nameless* office, I checked all four holes for poison. Then I made my choice.

It wasn't the best set I'd ever thrown. Head spins are harder when Malcolm X's ghost is screaming at you. No Black writer will get into *Nameless* again without at least three clean flares. But I could do swipes in my sleep and used back tucks to compensate for a general lack of charisma. The performance earned applause from a dozen picturesque women my age, which made things easier. I told myself it was about padding out my résumé.

The second call from *Nameless* came the next morning. I was hired, having demonstrated my passion for the industry through my zero years of fashion experience and an ill-fitting suit taken from my father. As an editorial intern, I was charged with writing only the best slander about Coco Chanel.

"This issue's theme is Legend. We'll call it the Legendary issue, and fill it with legends," Pandora explained in her best Don Draper impression.[9] "The towers of our culture. We won't limit legends to the past. We're

---

[7] **"Sound of Da Police"**: A seminal 1993 anti-police brutality anthem. Distinguished from N.W.A.'s "Fuck Da Police" in public memory by KRS-One's habit of weaving in and out of a Jamaican accent.

[8] **Bboy:** The in-community term for a break-dancer. Not to be confused with the similar term for a Blood gang member, lest one make unnecessary enemies.

[9] **Don Draper:** The protagonist of *Mad Men*, a popular drama about a 1950s ad agency. Noted rapscallion.

beyond that. We'll also focus on future and living legends, like Tiësto and Riff Raff." [10,11]

I started on Wednesday, and by Friday I wanted to leave for a fulfilling career selling my blood to back-alley doctors. I was fairly certain I was O-negative, or AB positive. The details didn't seem that important. With time and effort, I could work my way up to selling sperm and lesser organs. My left lung was just coasting off the effort of my right lung. It had the entitled shiftlessness Republicans crusaded against every two to four years.

Pandora's minions could be divided into two factions: the broken and the brainwashed. Anne was the queen of the second faction, convinced that Pandora would drive all the infidels out of Fashion Week and take the careers of the faithful to the promised land. As leader of the brainwashed, she was the first point of contact with the broken. We sat in the back, critiquing each other's résumés and writing samples.

I often shared a desk with a loyalist named Jenna. I hoped to create an understanding between our people, or even an alliance through marriage. She was more interested in turning Pandora into a steppingstone for her future. My approach to the work wasn't any less cynical, I just lacked confidence in Pandora's ability to keep this ship afloat for another year.

"You seem pretty frustrated," she said as I contemplated doing a side flip out the window. I might have gone for it if we were on a higher floor.

"Just a bit," I lied.

"Well, try to stick around. The last guy kicked a hole in the wall and left for 'lunch.' He never came back."

"I won't do that," I replied. For all of my ire, I knew I'd slither my way out of *Nameless*, not stomp. No direct confrontation with Pandora would end without a cameo by the NYPD. When people like her snapped their fingers, people like me disappeared behind a wall of nightsticks.

"Good, we have a chance to learn something here. We shouldn't waste it."

The typical day started with press releases. I converted messages from a curated set of publicists into *Nameless*'s signature glowing endorsements. This is distinct from advertising because it isn't. Even without my contribution, half our articles consisted of advertorials, the worst neologism since domino theory.[12] I usually burned through the press releases in an

---

[10] **Tiësto:** Trailblazing EDM DJ. I'll leave whether or not that's a good thing to history.

[11] **Riff Raff:** An eminently forgettable White hip-hop artist of the early 2010s. Decidedly non-legendary.

[12] **Domino theory:** The Cold War theory/military strategy/superstition espousing that one state falling to communism would rapidly lead to its neighbors falling to communism. Frequently cited as a defense of the Vietnam War.

hour, which convinced Pandora I was half-assing them. I was, so I started padding the process out with strategic visits to YouTube.

My game trailer marathons were occasionally interrupted by feature articles. Pandora assigned these through Anne, since directly addressing untouchables is forbidden for the upper castes. I needed to at least upgrade to a sweater vest before standing on the same carpet as Pandora Bastille. Or whatever they called her in the Midwest.

Nameless had a unique research method, which looked like plagiarism if you squinted. Anne walked me through creating an article about Lady Gaga's flying dress, Volantis, a news item we missed the bell on by about a week.[13] Volantis was the final consequence of a society with unlimited funds and a limited attention span. Our report was a chimera sewn together with parts from Vogue and a half-dozen small blogs. Anne asked how I wanted to sign it, and I adopted the pen name "Staff Writer."

Thanks to the efforts of people we'd call socialists today, Pandora couldn't do much to ruin lunch. In fact, she often made me appreciate it more by explaining to the entire room that she couldn't eat because of an incoming event. That might have been a cry for help, but my empathy required a full-time salary.

In any case, the website existed to support *the issue*. Pandora gave those words all the dramatic weight she could, fueled by an honest passion for print. These theatrics made the whole enterprise seem less grandiose and more quixotic. I don't think the Big Sean interview I transcribed and edited for *the issue* changed the course of fashion history.[14] I don't even think it changed the course of Big Sean's career. But playing and replaying his conversation with Pandora was the longest day of mine.

Since I'm already riding the slander train, here's a tidbit about Big Sean. He can talk. I don't mean in the patronizing "he's so well spoken" sense. I mean that Big Sean never shuts the hell up. Big Sean can talk about himself at a length that would give John Galt pause.[15] Big Sean can talk about himself until the microphone short-circuits. Big Sean can talk about himself

---

[13] **Volantis:** At the peak of her fame, pop musician and fashionista Lady Gaga commissioned and wore a flying (well, hovering) dress. The electric gown/vehicle served as a publicity stunt for the *ARTPOP* album release party. Time and energy that could have gone toward improving *ARTPOP*.

[14] **Big Sean:** The Detroit rapper behind "Dance (Ass)" and presumably a second song.

[15] **John Galt:** The objectivist Übermensch from Ayn Rand's novel *Atlas Shrugged*. Near the end of the novel he gives a speech roughly three times the length of the human attention span.

until the sun finally collapses into its own gravity well. Containing his songs to three standard verses is a triumph of human will.

The magazine spread used maybe a fifth of the transcript, and the extended online version had a third at most. Impressive, given the questions he worked with. Pandora Bastille gave interviews the way I performed heart transplants: stabbing at the dark, attempting to impersonate something seen on television. Each question meandered further than the last, turning the interview into a game of free association.

Pandora liked to break up the daily formula with stunt firings. These were more for the benefit of the remaining employees than the person in question. A firing began with a passive-aggressive touch, like a missing desktop or a name left out of a conversation. They ended in some variation of "You clearly don't understand what we're about." This meant I was doomed: I didn't understand what we were about either. To the credit of New York's aspiring fashionistas, only one of them cried.

Occasionally, we had celebrity guests between firings. Then Pandora demonstrated the only two skills I ever observed from her: photography and brown-nosing. If you returned Pandora's calls, you were on the A-list. My favorite incident was in November, after I'd resolved to quit. I was halfway through a muted round of *Civilization IV* when Pandora scurried toward the door.[16] It was the fastest I'd ever seen her move. I'm surprised she didn't trip over her own dog.

Pandora led a distracted-looking man into the room. She stopped him in the middle to show the peasantry the light she'd brought into their lives.

"This is Such-and-such! He's very famous in Australia, and blowing up all over the U.S."

I'd never seen Such-and-such in my life, and his name escapes me now. That's not a diss: I simply had a narrow cultural awareness that started on BBC and ended on 4chan. The best way to gain my attention was to argue with Barack Obama or a fourteen-year old.

"Dennard, Jenna, you're into alternative music! You must be thrilled."

"Yeah!" said Jenna. I opened a packet of raisins.

"Do you have any questions for him?"

"So many! I don't know where to begin!" said Jenna. I ate a handful of raisins.

"That's fine, we need to finish the photoshoot first anyway. Clear out of the back, I need to set up the camera." Her eyes promised that we'd be flayed later.

---

[16] ***Civilization IV***: A nation-management simulator that should be mandatory for incoming presidents.

Before tripping into publishing, Pandora was a fashion photographer. Despite my hope that she'd share a cell in hell with Ronald Reagan, I had to admit that she was good at it.[17] Everyone she photographed had a look that made you want to spend money.

But there are limits to everyone's powers. After setting up her camera, she handed Such-and-such an outfit. It looked like someone tried to make a bat costume out of ostrich feathers, and he knew it. Such-and-such stared at his reflection in naked horror. The aesthetic was somewhere between failed cosplay and Syfy original movie.

"It's from the designer that made Lady Gaga's outfits," Pandora explained. Such-and-such tried to look excited, while Jenna eyed the floor. My interest was finally engaged, so I put the raisins aside.

"Oh. Great!" said Such-and-such.

Such-and-such faced the camera with a veteran's distant stare. Each pose made him look more like Zeus had his way with a seagull than the last. The vest's feathers tended to shed, giving the prerequisite "crawling on the ground" shot the appearance that he'd fallen from a great height.

I don't know if these shots were featured in *the issue.* After finally enjoying a day at work, I jumped ship. The *Nameless* experience had peaked. I no longer have access to my undergraduate email account, but the letter looked something like this.

Dear Scarecrow,

I've contracted a disease that can only be treated by day-drinking Irish Car Bombs.[18] I'm afraid this will keep me from finishing our work on the Legendary issue, which is set to change the way we think about Miley Cyrus knockoffs for the next twenty minutes. Though I may not be with you in body or spirit, you'll always have the smoldering seed of resentment I left behind. Along with the assorted wads of gum I hid throughout the office.

Sincerely,
Probably Bernard

Two months later, I started dating a Fashion Institute of Technology student. I asked if she read *Nameless.* She looked at me like I'd made the name up. I showed her a glossy copy of *the issue*, which failed to impress.

---

[17] **Ronald Reagan:** The 40th president of the United States and the principle figure behind Reaganomics, 1980s Cold War escalation, and the Iran–Contra scandal. In short, conservative icon and liberal bogeyman. You can guess which camp I fall into.

[18] **Irish Car Bombs:** An undergraduate-favorite drink in which Irish cream and whiskey are dropped into a stout. Do not order this in Dublin.

I still have that issue on my bookshelf, between *Cryptonomicon* and a risqué coloring book.[19] In hindsight, the name is the key to understanding Pandora. She had the idiot courage to call it *Nameless* without a hint of irony or acknowledgement of a preexisting literary magazine with the same name. Because more than anything, she wanted to stay cool. Pandora was in a death match against time with predictable results. Whatever she hired, fired, hyped, implanted, or promoted, she drifted a little further from hip every day.

I doubt she stopped chasing that dragon. I imagine her somewhere in Soho, dressing a rapper named Lil' Bigplanet like a bird of paradise. Hopefully she enjoys it.

[19] ***Cryptonomicon***: A Neal Stephenson historical fiction novel about World War II, codebreaking, treasure hunters, morphine addiction, the 1940s Japanese psyche, and relationships. It's a trip.

CONQUERING CONCORD

LUISA REYES

My colleague was hesitating, and I was a bit puzzled as to why. For with our pattern of color coordinating our professional attire, in the past few weeks we had managed to establish ourselves as quite the power pair at the various business and chambers of commerce meetings throughout the Cambridge and Boston, Massachusetts, area. We were both still feeling the lingering effects of the 2008 economic downturn that haunted the job market, finding ourselves in the most unenviable position of being unemployed attorneys. However, despite this undesirable status of ours, we were making the best of things by doing pro bono trademark, nonprofit boards, and other light legal work for our high-society Creole boss.

As the founder of an exclusive and upscale bed-and-breakfast network, our boss combined her skills developed from her MBA studies at Harvard University with her New Orleans-influenced taste for elegance. Consequently, her three-story home in Cambridge was decorated with ornate antiques obtained from local estate sales. And our "headquarters," as my colleague referred to the home, featured a grand piano and a gilded harp. Quite the refreshing change from the blandly decorated bare white walls coupled with grey-toned cubicles mainstay of a corporate office. And given our success at establishing a good reputation for ourselves in the past few weeks, it definitely seemed like this more creative environment had a positive effect on us as we represented our boss's company throughout the New England region.

Yet, as we prepared to attend the Concord Chamber of Commerce meeting this sunny afternoon, my colleague was stalling as best as she could. While normally we either walked to the business meetings we attended or were chauffeured by our boss's husband, since Concord was a bit farther away, today I would be the one doing the driving. And with the grandfather clock ticking away, I found myself unable to come up with a logical explanation for my colleague's out-of-character reluctance. But, not wanting to needlessly harm our commendable reputation, I finally declared that it was past time for us to make our commute to Concord, leading to my irresolute colleague relenting and the two of us piling into my car and heading northwest up the road to Concord.

Along the way we made some small talk about our backgrounds. With me hailing originally from Tuscaloosa, Alabama, we talked about Southern belles and other folksy aspects of Southern culture. Our Creole boss often expressed a longing for her Southern state of Louisiana. Which, truthfully, I found to be unexpected since Cambridge, with its pride in being the most opinionated ZIP code in the nation, seemed like a better fit for such a well-educated, accomplished, and intelligent African American lady. However, much to my surprise, my Midwestern colleague also showed some excitement about Southern-American culture by letting it be known that she and her sister had some Southern roots a couple of generations back. After pulling into Concord, I promptly parked my car and we walked into the rather inconspicuously small building that housed this afternoon's chamber of commerce meeting.

Immediately upon entering the office space, I noticed that we were indeed a tad late. Everybody was preparing to gather around in a circle and make their introductions. And a tall, slender receptionist, who appeared to be perhaps approaching her mid-forties, greeted us at the door with that unique type of hostile smile that harbored a definite "don't mess with me" warning in the forcefully upturned corners of the edges of her lips—a detail I thought odd and more akin with the aging Southern sorority women from back home.

But we'll win her over, I told myself, as I optimistically asked for a pen to sign in with.

She paused and looked at me for a moment before deciding it was OK to hand me an insignificant plastic ballpoint pen of the type that comes in a pack of ten that can be purchased at a cheap big-box store for the astounding price of two simple dollars. It was a pen she had been holding in her hand, and I found it peculiar and maybe a bit unprofessional that they didn't just have a pen placed on the sign-in sheet that was available for everyone to use.

However, shrugging these oddities off to the side, when I finished signing both my name and that of the company we represented, I nonchalantly passed it on to my colleague for her to use. This gesture provoked the lady's contentious smile to spread to a look of barely restrained incredulity and led me to conclude that the character of this chamber of commerce meeting was by far the most unusual one we had encountered.

Once the unexpected hassle of signing in was complete, we took our places in the circle and the introductions began. The man representing the local theater group proudly boasted that he could trace his history all the way back to Louisa May Alcott of *Little Women* fame. And the lady whose bakery was offering the refreshments explained that she did include gluten-free options. A fact I delighted in, since I'm gluten-free. Then there was a man with a tour group, and he and the theater man began discussing possibilities for a mutual business venture. One lady, who hailed from Ohio, explained that she was having some severe health issues, prompting everyone to boast of the good healthcare available in Boston. Only for her to explain that in Ohio they have the Cleveland Clinic, which offers world-class healthcare. For the most part, the businesses being represented that evening were rather small compared with the ones we'd encountered in other places. But the introductions went so well that, by the conclusion of the formal part of the meeting, by all outward appearances, everyone seemed to be very upbeat and at ease with one another.

Afterwards, while partaking of some of the refreshments, we encountered a fellow who was a huge Michigan fan. And after I explained to him that my colleague was from Michigan, he immediately struck up a conversation with her about Michigan college football. Indeed, he very excitedly took us to his back office to show off all of his autographed Michigan memorabilia. I stood by silently while he and my colleague reveled in Paradise as they exchanged cheers of "Go Blue!" in between assurances from him that he had all of our business materials and would be seriously considering them. In an unabated state of euphoria over encountering a fellow Michigan fan in the Northeast, he kept us in his office at length, which didn't go unnoticed by the others present at the Concord Chamber of Commerce meeting, resulting in us being some of the last to leave with everyone making a point to speak to us and encouraging us to make sure and attend the next month's meeting as well.

It simply couldn't have gone any better! I thought to myself while driving us back to our stylish headquarters. For, despite that curiously awkward moment with the receptionist, we had conquered Concord and were both just radiating with contentment. Later that evening, as I drafted our required summary of the meeting, I wrote glowingly about how my colleague had just made a new best friend and how we were so welcome at the meeting.

"Did you read your colleague's report?" was my boss's unusually succinct response, after I sent it in.

No, I thought to myself. Why should I? We had both agreed that the evening had been a splendid one, and there wasn't any room for debate on the matter. But, eventually, my natural curiosity set in and took over, so I began reading her report. And my two full lips split as my mouth fell open in a state of unanticipated shock.

My colleague explained in detail how, as the sole African American present at a previous meeting of the Concord Chamber of Commerce, she had been accused of stealing the pen for the sign-in sheet. I was aghast.

Is she writing about the same meeting we just attended? I asked myself. For prior to this summary of hers, I had no indication that she had ever been to Concord before.

I am actually half Mexican, myself. But, with this being a decade prior to the Trump era's slogan of "Build that wall!" my Hispanic heritage didn't cause people to quake in fear. Instead, people commented approvingly about what "hard workers Mexicans are" and how "well they work with their hands," and I was often mistaken for being of Italian or French heritage due to my fair skin coupled with my long dark hair and eyes. This enabled me to pass as mainstream without any effort on my part while attending these meetings and pursuing my academic studies.

I reread my colleague's words for any kind of an indication that she was referring to someplace else, but it was in vain and out of an effort to refuse facing reality. After all, this was the Obama era. A time filled with the ingenuous illusion of having righted all the social ills of past centuries. And the resurgence of ideas long thought dead, but merely lying dormant until the Trump administration, was unforeseen. However, suddenly, the recollection of the hostile smile of the receptionist "greeting" us when we first entered the office space in Concord manifested itself clearly in my head. My colleague further explained in her summary how, during her previous visit, the receptionist and others had let it be known that she was never welcome back. She wrote that she had actually felt tremulous at the thought of returning.

"Whoa!" I exhaled out loud while leaning back in my chair completely overcome by a weighty disbelief. *Have I fallen into a time warp and suddenly found myself reading something from my Deep South home state before the 1960s civil rights era?*

I looked around to be sure. The Longfellow House, where the renowned poet once lived, was still up the way only a couple of blocks. Harvard Square, the triangular plaza adjacent to Harvard Yard of Harvard University lore, was still but a brisk walk away. And with Massachusetts's legal approval of same-sex marriage in 2004 still fresh on everybody's minds, some men were kissing each other unabashedly on the corner of the street.

But this is Boston, I thought to myself, as I kept fighting the notion that such things as what my colleague had experienced before I came along were indeed a reality. Yet, upon finishing reading my colleague's report, I found myself contemplating things in a way I never would have thought possible.

For "Boston is the bastion of all things liberal" is a frequent slogan repeated back home in Alabama and one that I called to mind while pinching myself some more. Just to make sure that I was indeed living in the modern era.

But then it dawned on me: Boston has its own history of race riots during the school desegregation era, and many of the New England states were opposed to the women's suffrage amendment for fear they would lose their cheap factory labor force. What my colleague was saying certainly couldn't be true in such a forward-thinking place . . . or could it?

The answer is a resounding yes.

Those who deny the existence of White privilege like to point to the White poverty rate, which, by the way, is half that of the Black poverty rate. But poverty isn't the opposite of privilege. The opposite of privilege is going to look at a house that's for sale and having it suddenly taken off the market once the sellers see you. The opposite of privilege is chauffeuring a client in a BMW to a high-end office building and having the people run and hide because they aren't used to your kind being there. The opposite of privilege is being in a room full of people and being the one singled out as having whisked away the cheap sign-in pen, merely because you are the only one of a different skin color present. If that meeting in Concord taught me anything, it's that we must work to ensure that our modern-day, progressive society is not merely an image but, rather, substantive enough to withstand the scrutiny of future generations

THE MONOLINGUAL ASPECT OF WHITENESS AT WORK

JAVIER SÁNCHEZ

In his introduction to *After Whiteness: Unmaking an American Majority*, author and literary critic Mike Hill quotes American poet William Carlos Williams to suggest one of his principal arguments: "No whiteness is so white as the memory of whiteness" (Hill 2004, 1).[1] Recapping his experience at the American Renaissance conference in 2002, Hill explains how participants nostalgically mourned the loss of the White race as the leading and most authentic essence of American identity (citizens of The United States of America).[2] Although this death of whiteness in the United States is later disproven by Hill, those at the conference sought to consolidate their solidarity to continue the dream of racial purity against the pluralistic, diverse element of the nation. By following such a strategy, that is, arguing its extinction to justify its revival, they purposely created a vacuum, an absence, from which to reinstate whiteness after their imaginary loss. According to Hill, the move to declare the passing of whiteness implies both a surrender of it in favor of a multicultural fate and, at the same time, an effective defense for whiteness from a location of displacement. Hence, conference participants readily appropriated arguments that had been used previously by minorities and marginalized groups to contest hegemonic cultural and political practices. By placing themselves outside the majority (as they perceived whiteness to be in the minority), they immediately called to preserve what they understood to be solely and genuinely American (USA). Therefore, questions of immigration, public policy, crime, interracial relationships, public higher education, census methods or racial categorization, labor practices and the importance of both English studies and whiteness

[1] Dr. Mike Hill is an associate professor of English at SUNY Albany. He publishes on eighteenth-century studies, critical race theory and contemporary cultural studies.

[2] *American Renaissance* is an online publication founded and edited by the controversial figure Jared Taylor. Moreover, *American Renaissance* holds a conference every year (since 1994). The Southern Poverty Law Center has catalogued this association as a hate group.

studies become particularly relevant to delineate and reinstate their view of the nation-state. From this standpoint and based on the "memory of whiteness," nostalgic supporters brought forth a forceful regeneration of whiteness that intended to take the nation back to its supposedly White and pure origins.

Within this context, that of an imagined loss of whiteness, and using an approach similar to Hill's, I propose that we think about a key component missing in *After Whiteness: Unmaking an American Majority*, namely language. More specifically, I would like to reflect on the role of languages in academia where we witness the argument regarding the demise of whiteness (in theory if not in practice) but also the case for its regeneration. What I suggest is that "the memory of White" carries with it an implicit, strong and intrinsic connection to what perhaps we could term "the memory of English." Thus, any assertion of whiteness, in my view, implies a defense of the English language as a crucial element of U.S. American identity as understood by White, monolingual, English speakers inside and outside of academia. Basically, I wish to link the concept of whiteness to the English language and, more particularly, I intend to associate whiteness with monolingual speakers of English (both professors and administrators) within academia. Moreover, I would like to show some of the repercussions of this implicit and explicit defense of monolingualism (English based) as part of the whiteness concept for all foreign-language-related matters in higher education institutions in the USA, including language offerings and other initiatives. I hope to demonstrate a contradiction. In spite of well-intended proposals by administrators and professors to be more inclusive, and despite all the discussions about the importance to internationalize the curriculum, notwithstanding the efforts toward globalization in higher education, what repeatedly prevails is the cutting of language programs and, just as problematic, the approach to teaching students about our multicultural world *in English*. The message we send to our students, consciously or not, is that learning foreign languages is not necessary in a world where English reigns supreme. This is indeed an extension of whiteness.

In his discussion on race and White America, Hill recalls the image of Eve on the cover of *Time* magazine. Eve, Hill explains, is "the computer-generated multiracial cover girl for *Time* magazine's 1993 special issue, 'The New Face of America.' Eve…is a composite image of fourteen different racial and ethnic identities, digitally morphed into a muted picture of the nation's uncharted post-white future" (Hill 2004, 9). Certainly, a number of issues must be considered regarding this illustration. There is the obvious biblical connotation of her name—pointing to a new beginning. Critics have also alluded to her as a type of Frankenstein, as if made of various functioning parts. And, on the opposite view, the image is interpreted as a suggestion of a happy future of mixed races.[3] According to Hill, Eve's message "might be that this future, like Eve herself, is for the first time not self-evidently present to the nation that struggles to claim it." In other words, the uncertain future of White America is fully represented in this image where the mixing of racial attributes dilutes whiteness. A sense of belonging and ownership lessens as fear increases because the mirror-image is diverse, multiracial and not fully White. But about Eve and her connection to languages? Specifically, I am interested in posing the question "What *languages* does she speak?" Will a multicultural, diverse, multiracial society also be multilingual? Or will Eve be limited to speaking English regardless of her cultural heritages (as suggested by the composite image)? Is Eve monolingual? Will the English-only attitude be a reductionist normative element to encase all cultures?

Much has been said about the death of the English-language-based Western canon in departments of literature across universities. If the Western canon was traditionally formed mostly by White, male, British and American writers, recent discussions (and some actions) to diversify literary studies have fallen rather short. The intended move towards multiculturalism in literary studies and the impact of cultural studies has not diminished the prevalence of the Western canon in academia. Hill notes that the 1995 *Modern Language Association of America* (MLA) report indicates the following: "For the American survey, the top five authors [are] Hawthorne (66 percent), followed by Whitman, Dickinson, Twain, and Emerson. For the British survey [the studied authors are] Chaucer (89 percent), Shakespeare, Milton, Wordsworth, Pope and Donne. By contrast, James Baldwin, Langston Hughes and Alice Walker are cited with frequencies of less than 1 percent" (Hill 2004, 209). This MLA report shows that the Western canon remains dominantly White, male and English. Hill goes on to argue that "color [can] save the canon" (viii) by consistently including authors such as Toni Morrison. Considered an American (USA) classic by many, her work offers the often-forgotten or disregarded topic of U.S. American slavery, its consequences and its lingering effects on the present.[4]

---

[3] See *After Whiteness: Unmaking an American Majority* by author Mike Hill pages 9–10.

[4] In *Playing in the Dark: Whiteness and the Literary Imagination*, Toni Morrison refers to a "certain set of assumptions accepted among literary historians and critics [namely] that traditional, canonical American literature is free of, uninformed, and unshaped by the four-hundred-year-old presence of, first, Africans and then African-Americans in the United States." Morrison critiques this tacit agreement exposing that "American literature has been clearly the preserve of White male views, genius,

This topical absence in the U.S. American and European canon offerings is blatant. Moreover, I also think that the Western canon can and should evolve not only through the inclusion of color but by studying literary works in their original languages. Allowing students to read (and discuss) works by, for example, Dante Alighieri, Nathalie Sarraute, Ana María Matute, Isak Dinesen or Miguel de Cervantes as part of the Western canon in their original languages would signal the value of diverse languages and their cultures. Courses on great canonical works are taught in English (as the lingua franca) for all students, but those students with the desire and skill to read such books in their original languages would benefit greatly.[5] And if we are restricted to the British/American canon, why not emphasize and read authors' writing in languages other than English (Spanish and Creole, for example)? From this perspective, Latino writers offer American topics in English, Spanish and Spanglish.[6] This approach would allow both color and language to contrast the predominance of whiteness and English. It is a view that would require an extensive rethinking and reworking of our language, literature and humanities divisions in higher education institutions across the U.S.

Realizing a short-term plan however would be much simpler. To avoid the monolingual aspect of whiteness as a restrictive instrument within academia, the support for language programs, departments, professors and offerings is a necessary step, as is the integration of foreign languages across the university's curriculum. This humble suggestion has encountered quite limited backing as language departments across the nation face the

---

and power." She also argues that "[t]he contemplation of this black presence is central to any understanding of our national literature and should not be permitted to hover at the margins of the literary imagination" (4–5).

[5] Part of the problem lies in our own insecurities as educators unfamiliar with other languages. Based on my experience as a student, monolingual professors tended to evade comments, views or interpretations grounded in texts not translated into English. Even if we do not know the original language of the work we teach, students with that particular knowledge can be an asset in the classroom by conducting proper (if not specialized) comparative analysis of texts and bringing forward subtleties and nuances of interpretation based on the two different languages of study.

[6] Authors who use different languages in their writing include Rolando Hinojosa–Smith, Sandra Cisneros and Roberto Fernández, among many others. Creole literature is also highly relevant yet overlooked. See *Louisiana Creole Literature: A Historical Study* by Catharine Savage Brosman. Famous bilingual or multilingual authors who have been part of the canon include Vladimir Nabokov, Joseph Conrad, Jack Kerouac, Samuel Beckett, Milan Kundera. Canadian writers could easily be part of the American (continent) canon if we consider their bilingual abilities. Yann Martel is one such author.

presumed unnecessary prejudice and its serious consequences. In point of illustration, I will trace this topic in essays published by *The Chronicle of Higher Education* and the *Modern Language Association of America*. Professor of comparative literature Mary Louise Pratt published in 2003 an article titled "Building a New Public Idea About Language." Writing against the notion that the United States of America is a "cementerio de lenguas" (a language cemetery), she reminds us of the great number of languages spoken in this country.[7] Indeed, she proposes that we take full advantage of our rich, linguistic diversity by creating "opportunities to develop bilingualism and bi-literacy in native and non-native speakers alike, opportunities to nurture the linguistically capable diplomats, scholars and international professionals we so conspicuously need as well as opportunities to create bilingual professionals able to work with and among domestic populations." In order to accomplish this, Pratt argues, a new understanding of languages must be attained, where monolingualism is the handicap and where local heritage communities in the country become key players to form a diverse, multilingual future for our nation. However, this new public idea about language remains unrealized.

In fact, evidence of systematically undermining the value of forming multilingual citizens and students abounds. Professor of French Catherine Porter gave the MLA presidential address in 2009 titled "English is Not Enough." She argued to maintain the emphasis and importance given to English, but she asked, "What leads us to suppose that English alone is *enough* for Americans" despite the fact that multilingualism is the reality in our global community? What Porter defends as the highest benefit of learning languages is the following: "Access to the full richness and complexity of human experience…differences in perception, understanding and communicative relations" (552). And yet, the 2018 MLA report on enrollments in languages other than English in U.S. institutions of higher education shows that, "between fall 2013 and fall 2016, enrollments in languages other than English fell 9.2% in colleges and universities," the second largest decline in history (1–2). This precipitous decline in enrollments, according to the report prepared by Dennis Looney and Natalia Lusin, confirms a downward trend rather than an anomaly. The decrease in foreign language interest is, in my view, a symptom of a larger condition that has to do with higher-level politics based on instilling whiteness via devaluing other languages and promoting English-only viewpoints. Certainly, politicians help promote a particular public perception about

7 According to the U.S. Census Bureau, there are at least 350 languages spoken in the country. See census.gov/newsroom/press-releases/2015/cb15-185.html.

languages with their attitudes. Taking as an example the case Lucy Ferriss presents in her "The Privilege of Language," we know about then-Governor Matt Bevin of Kentucky declaring his opposition to funding the humanities curricula with public money. Bevin cited the French language and even literature as nonessential fields of study to obtain employment. Ferriss indeed maintains that, "[w]ith the blinkered attitude available only to those for whom the world's lingua franca is their mother tongue, we insist on the essential requirement of learning English even as we downgrade the importance of Americans' learning other languages [and yet] woe betide the student or aspiring employee who cannot communicate in English." The denial of funding, degrading the study of languages in general and expressing denigrating opinions about languages other than English are examples of whiteness at work across all of society.

Nonetheless, the research indicates that leaders and administrators in higher education pay great attention to labor demand to offer marketable programs.[8] A peculiar case is that of the former North Georgia College and State University (now the University of North Georgia). In 2005, the institution added Chinese to its current offerings of Spanish, French and German. As Julian Wyllie writes, North Georgia was "one of six senior military colleges in the country [and], the university now has about 5 percent of its students in the Reserve Officers' Training Corps" (2). Being so, and given the need, based on national security concerns, to have officers understand and speak Chinese, the U.S. Defense Department allowed the university to access money for the study of critical languages through Project Global Officer. The $3.2 million donation made it possible for the institution to expand its language institutes, study abroad opportunities, language offerings and, consequently, its enrollments. Despite the success of this instance, two concerns arise. First, the need to study what is called a critical language may change according to various political, economic and social circumstances and the funding could disappear quite precipitously. And second, learning languages only to fill a particular job description, as Ferriss and Pratt also indicate in their essays, delineates a very narrow approach (which, in addition, may be based on fear if learning a language is linked to military undertakings). Knowing languages appears to be valid in cases of near emergency and, as a norm, we fail to understand what Porter described in her MLA speech as a key benefit of learning languages: "Access to the full richness and complexity of human experience…and communicative relations" (Porter 2010, 552). The economic recession of

[8] "Higher Education Year in Review." 2018. *Hanover Research*. New York: Hanover Research.

2008 proves it. According to Steven Johnson, 651 foreign language programs were lost in only three years. As he writes in *The Chronicle of Higher Education*: "A 2014 report showed that the recession hit foreign-language degree programs harder than it did many other humanities programs. In the immediate aftermath, colleges cut 12 percent of foreign-language degree programs compared with 6 percent of all degree programs" (Johnson 2019, 3). The reality of the situation is that language learning stands as a second-class citizen facing an English-is-enough mentality.

The value of language learning in my current institution is relative. Nestled in the Pine Barrens, a predominantly White, conservative South Jersey area, Stockton University still retains some of the 1960s idealism that was prevalent when the institution was founded as Stockton State College in 1969. As described by Professor Bill Daly, Stockton intends to "make available to state college students at state college prices the kind of interdisciplinary and individualized liberal arts instruction…usually reserved for students at the most selective and expensive private liberal arts colleges" (Daly 2011, vii). The fundamental idea was (and still is) to offer a liberal arts transformational experience to their students at affordable prices. Over the years, the institution has undergone many changes but noteworthy are the consolidation of the four major pillars that define the institution at the moment: learning, engagement, sustainability and global perspectives. Of all those pillars, the fourth initiative remains highly underdeveloped. The global perspectives mission of the university is described as follows: "We envision laying the foundation of our global theme by building a community capable of developing opportunities to collaborate across a diverse world of cultures, race, gender, orientation, and age, one that prepares us for global participation" (Keenan 2011, 162). But inconsistencies and contradictions abound between the mission statement and its reality. This is what I intend to show below with two major examples. Central to the presentation of this view is the idea that despite a well-articulated plan to internationalize our institution, language programs seem an afterthought since the globalization initiative is invariably done solely in English. In fact, the argument could be made that internationalization means "allowing" all other peoples and cultures to know about and adapt to White U.S. American culture and the English language. While claiming to prepare students for a global environment, promoting the study of other languages and cultures continues to be dismal.

The first example I wish to share relates to the writing across the curriculum requirement at our institution. Since 1978, students have been required to take a minimum of three (later this requirement increased to four) courses with W attributes (a course with a writing component where a

W1 is a highly intensive writing course and a W2 is less intensive but nonetheless amply rigorous. A W2 course shows commitment to teaching and writing. A W1 course shows commitment to teaching the craft of writing). The intention is to guarantee that students acquire significant practice in writing before they graduate. I find this enterprise extremely laudable, and I am proud to say that the Writing Program received the G. Theodore Mitau Award for Innovation and Change in Higher Education in 1984. Eager and willing to participate as a faculty member, I read the Writing Program manual to comply with requirements and to prepare my courses properly before applying for the W attribute. The policy reads as follows: "A college-wide commitment to writing…writing is an essential intellectual tool…All faculty are invited to participate in the Writing Program…W1 and W2 courses [can be] offered in *all disciplines* [and by] all divisions" [my emphasis]. After reading this inclusive language, I crafted two of my advanced-level (third-year, Spanish-major) courses.[9] I applied for a W1 to be assigned to "Advanced Spanish Language Composition and Syntax" and a W2 for "Advanced Oral and Written Expression in Spanish."

The Writing Program did *not* approve those W attributes, and a long (academic year 2007–2008) discussion involving the Languages and Culture Studies Program, the Writing Program and the dean of arts and humanities ensued. The email(s) I received indicating the denial stated that "your courses do not merit W designations…The Writing Program will only approve new courses that include *writing in English* as W courses… Approving courses in languages other than English as W2 courses might especially prevent students whose native language is not English from working on their writing in English" (my emphasis). Reading these answers, I quickly understood that the issue was not writing itself, but rather the language of instruction. I was proposing to teach composition in Spanish,

[9] Extensive and various guidelines on written assignments were given to students for these courses as part of the syllabi. I briefly summarize my approach to teaching writing here: "The writing element of the course is essential. We will pay special attention to the following elements: design of a paragraph, active voice versus passive voice, affirmative and negative statements, usage of definite and concrete language, precision of vocabulary, link words for transitions, organization of ideas, consistency of tenses, telling the plot versus creating an argument, thinking about the reader, usage of sophisticated vocabulary and syntax. There will be revision and peer editing of your essays before you give your paper to the professor. Follow peer editing forms provided. We will discuss format and necessary guidelines for writing papers in class. Special office hours will be determined for students to discuss writing issues with the professor. These assignments are intended to help us become familiar with your strengths and weaknesses in writing so that you may improve your language ability…"

that is, teaching syntax, proper grammar, construction of sentences, presenting a clear thesis, crafting of paragraphs, introductions, conclusions, use of supporting evidence, the avoidance of repetitions in vocabulary and ideas, the development of a strong argument, use of concise language and, of course, all of it using Spanish as the language of instruction. What was terrifyingly clear was that professors could get credit for their work, and add W designations to their courses, so long as they taught in English. Other languages did not "merit" it. Those teaching in languages other than English would be marginalized. I was now having to defend my profession, my expertise and, as a nontenured assistant professor, I faced the choice to participate or not in a form of explicit and dominant linguistic imperialism.

The Languages and Culture Studies Program and the school/division dean presented a vast array of arguments in favor of W designations to be approved for language courses (not just Spanish, but all language courses). I will name a few of these arguments here: Writing can be taught in any language, those skills are transferable to writing in another language, and a comparative or contrastive linguistic approach is greatly beneficial for students as they acquire a deeper understanding of their first language; language professors are specialists in teaching writing (and all communicative skills: speaking, reading, listening and writing). Denying W attributes for language courses effectively blocks experts from exercising and transmitting their knowledge to students. Moreover, language professors are not monolingual specialists; rather, most are bilingual or multilingual. If the Writing Program wishes to increase the number of W courses needed for students to graduate, they can do so; but excluding language courses from offering W attributes causes lower enrollments in the Languages and Culture Studies Program (students need W courses to graduate and will not take language courses without such designations). And, effectively, sends a clear message that other languages are less important than English at our institution and beyond. The political and ideological implications of this policy are blatant; also, quite important is the fact that the constant discourse about the importance to internationalize our curriculum seems vapid. Part of my goal as a professor of languages and literatures (I hold a comparative literature degree) is to prepare students to be successful (culturally, linguistically and professionally) in our global, multicultural and multilingual community. Emphasizing only English forces and restricts the academy to see and portray the world through the (valid but) particularly limited and incomplete perspective that White U.S. culture and English affords. In doing so, we reinforce the patronizing mechanism of defining the Other (regardless of good intentions) from a restricted location of knowledge because we do not have access to the understanding of Others. Among discussions for diversity, and conversations about embracing a pluralistic society in academia, what is constantly reinstated is the supremacy of the English language as an extension of whiteness.

The argument to exclude language courses from being assigned W attributes was untenable for the Writing Program. The dean showed his support and declared that "Not only is this a bad policy with regard to teaching writing [pedagogically speaking], it is politically objectionable."[10] After a long year of debate, the Writing Program still did not change its policy, although administrators stated that a revision of it would be appropriate. The spokesperson for the Writing Program sent me an email that dissolved the situation provisionally. He wrote: "The Writing Program met last week and agreed to grant [your courses] W designations, although it does not fit the college's standard understanding of the term (because the students are not writing in English). ...We also note that this is an [advanced] level course taken by a small number of students, so that making an exception for this course[s] does not worry us much." And so, an exception was made because only a few students would be affected. Instead of forcefully intending to include the value of all languages in the Writing Program, English prevailed in the guise of a benevolent patriarch. And, even if the intended purpose of the document stating the norms for the Writing Program was to teach students writing in English only, it does not exonerate its original authors. The document does not state anywhere that these regulations are for the *English* Writing Program. They simply assumed (and presumed all at Stockton would agree) that English was the only worthy, valid and necessary tool to teaching writing at the college.

The second example I present relates to the initiative I led to create a new interdisciplinary minor: Spanish for health and human services. I happily emphasize, again being proud of my university, that interdisciplinary approaches to teaching have been part of our institution since its inception. As Professor Linda Nelson has indicated, our commitment to a liberal arts education and our interdisciplinary methods allow "students to understand that knowledge is often constructed at points where disciplines intersect and not solely within the discrete theoretical boundaries of individual fields of knowledge" (Nelson 2011, 124). From this perspective, minors acquire great significance, according to Nelson, because students are "exposed to cultural practices and beliefs that depart significantly from…what [they] learned in their own enculturation" (124). Those pursuing an interdisciplinary minor would be able to "interrogate class, gender, and racial hegemonies" and reflect about "challenges inherent in a multicultural society" (124).

[10] Email communication during the spring of 2008.

Under this prerogative, a great number of interdisciplinary minors are offered, and we can approach any given topic from a historical, literary, sociological, scientific discipline or any other. And yet, once again, what is blatantly missing is the role of languages. With the exception of the Latin American and Caribbean studies minor (courses taught in Spanish on these topics count toward the minor) and the historical studies major, all others have not added any language component to their curricula.[11] And, so, majors and minors alike in business, global studies, Holocaust and genocide studies, migration studies, hospitality and tourism studies, and many others are not required any language study. Nonetheless, to curb the need for bilingual professionals in the health sciences professions, I proposed an interdisciplinary Spanish for health and human services minor where health topics would be taught by bilingual professors in the division of health sciences for the benefit of advanced-level students of Spanish majoring in health sciences. The marketplace demand for healthcare professionals and those who speak Spanish makes one think such a minor would receive wholehearted support.

The 30-page document I provided gave the curriculum committee ample information on demographics, professional needs, resources needed, as well as professors able and willing to teach the courses, including signatures from faculty and deans in health sciences and in arts and humanities, which courses were required and much pertinent information justifying the minor. A very brief summary of the courses proposed included a total of five courses: two required at the intermediate level of proficiency, "Spanish for Health and Human Services I" and "Spanish for Health and Human Services II," along with one advanced course, "Spanish and Global Health." Furthermore, to complete the proposed minor, students could take two or more courses at the advanced/superior level of proficiency: "Introduction to

[11] The case of the Literature Program at Stockton University is interesting. As Professor Thomas Kinsella acknowledges, "a four-semester foreign language component was added, at least in part to quell rising numbers" between the years 2003 and 2007 (123). However, as the humanities face low enrollments nowadays, students in the Literature Program are given various options to complete their language requirement. Instead of the four-semester language requirement, students could complete an interdisciplinary culture studies minor in Africana studies, Holocaust and genocide studies, global studies, Jewish studies, Latin American and Caribbean studies or women's, gender and sexuality studies. Students could also take the oral proficiency interview to demonstrate intermediate level of proficiency according to the American Council on the Teaching of Foreign Languages. Courses for these interdisciplinary culture studies minors are taught in English. The only exception is Latin American and Caribbean studies since courses taught in Spanish on those topics are allowed.

Health Sciences in Spanish," "Medical Terminology for Health in Spanish" and "Colombia: Culture and Society." This last course was designed for students and faculty in health sciences participating in the yearly faculty-led program to Bogotá. There, students visit clinics, hospitals and orphanages and interact with faculty members of the Universidad del Rosario and health science professionals in the capital of Colombia. We believed this last course to be crucial for our students traveling to South America as part of their studies. Our students, we hoped, would be advanced learners of Spanish able to communicate in Spanish and conduct research there. We wanted to empower them rather than assume their English would be enough or to think that the Colombians would know English. In addition, Spanish and Latin American culture and civilization courses would be accepted for the minor, as we believed that knowing the cultures of those countries would be advantageous. The goal was to help students achieve high levels of cultural and linguistic proficiency so that they could become efficient, well-rounded professionals abroad and in the U.S. It is for good reason that the health sciences division offers courses in speech, hearing, phonetics, language development and audiology in addition to cultural diversity in health care. The disadvantages for monolingual students would be significant when compared with bilingual graduates, especially considering the demand for bilingual professionals in the New York/New Jersey area.

The minor was *not* approved by the curriculum committee, and, in fact it was denied three times. As I inquired about the reasons, I was consistently met with unsatisfactory answers. As is customary, I awaited direction to revise the proposal, yet I never received guidance to modify it properly for its future approval. Certainly, I felt the integration of languages via interdisciplinary methods failed. The chair of the curriculum committee wrote: "The committee believes that what can be marketed to students is the Spanish minor with an area of interest in Health Sciences…The committee does not merely pass through proposals with a rubber stamp…The committee acknowledges the value of coursework in Spanish for students going into the Health Sciences, but does not agree that it requires creating a new minor." In other words, as a Spanish minor already exists, a specialized, specific minor in Spanish for health, social work and human services does not warrant approval. Or, as I take it, languages other than English cannot be integrated with other disciplines. This denial essentially continues to relegate languages to an "area of interest" without full official recognition of their usefulness and value in our national and international community. Indeed, a previous email from the chair of the committee stated that "the committee recommends that the courses designed for Health Sciences be made an area of interest (or whatever administrative categorization is appropriate) in the existing Spanish minor." Rather, my intention was to integrate the study of health material and Spanish. The type of recognition I was seeking would hardly be obtained by being placed in "whatever administrative categorization is appropriate."

Troubling as well is that those professors teaching in languages other than English are never exempt from having to explain how literature, history, philosophy, cultures, health, art, literary criticism and any other given topic is also simultaneously taught in their courses.[12] The perception that knowledge, real knowledge, can only be transmitted via the English language remains vehemently enforced in U.S. academia. Peer faculty members implicitly and explicitly often judge our field of expertise, relegating us to basic language study. Students certainly internalize this impression, and it diminishes the potential access to the understanding of other cultures and peoples. The perception that English is enough and the expectation that citizens of other countries must adapt to our culture and language damage our own U.S. students since they will actually and effectively be left behind in our competitive, multilingual, diverse global community. But also, it creates severe social and political divisions. Assuming that English is enough while relating the English language to the concept of whiteness, many are tempted to believe that linguistic adaptation of the Other to English is a derivative of an inferior people adjusting to a racially superior culture and not a consequence of certain historical events or of a socially and culturally constructed idea. The perpetuation of whiteness continues in academia through the dis-privilege of languages.

I hope to have shown that the prevalence and supremacy of English in academia is connected to the reflection author Hill presents in his work *After Whiteness: Unmaking an American Majority*. The strategy delineated by Hill works for whiteness as well as English. The strengthening of whiteness

[12] Microaggressions deeply ingrained in the prejudices of what Mike Hill calls whiteness in U.S. culture abound in our world. After the 2016 United States national election, one of my students declared, "We cannot speak Spanish anymore," to which I responded, "We can always do so in my class." The Office of Global Engagement director in my institution defined my cultural faculty-led program trip to Spain "too touristy"—failing to understand the value of immersing students in the language and culture of Spain. My advanced-level Spanish language students demonstrated excellent skills in navigating the culture of the country and conducting all our academic and daily activities there in Spanish. Recently, Africana studies was created as a major but not a single course included in this new B.A. program will expose students to French, Arabic or any of the indigenous languages spoken there. It is indeed troubling that English, the language of one of the colonizers on that continent, will be again *exploring* the cultures of African people and their descendants of the diaspora.

studies and English studies at universities and colleges hardly suggests the extinction of whiteness. Moreover, and within this context, the English language appears as an insidious extension of whiteness. Indeed, English is considered by most faculty and administrators (consciously or not) as the language of knowledge in the United States. Monolingual colleagues in the administration as well as monolingual faculty members, whether well-intended or otherwise, enforce English supremacy by their actions, prejudices and committee work at the expense of all other languages. Presumed to be unnecessary, languages suffer deeply from a perception of being disposable especially during a financial crisis or when budget cuts take place. This assessment of languages as less essential both inside and outside of higher education institutions impedes their integration with other disciplines. The dubious resolution made by the Writing Program's granting W designations to language courses as an exception and the curriculum committee's denial of the Spanish for health and human services interdisciplinary minor supports my perspective. The languages remain located at the margins, in a space of their own, and are expendable. The validity of languages is doubtful at best and in most cases an afterthought, even as universities nationwide discuss the dire need of internationalizing the curriculum to prepare students for our global community. Most of that work has been done in English, and of course (consciously or not) in the name of whiteness. What is needed to make our globalization objectives a reality is perhaps a renaissance of national support for the study of cultures through the medium of languages, of all languages, and not only English.

Sources

Brosman, C.S. 2013. *Louisiana Creole Literature: A Historical Study.* Jackson, Mississippi: University of Mississippi Press.

Daly, W. 2011. "Elite Education for State College Students." In *Reaching 40: The Richard Stockton College of New Jersey*, edited by Ken Tompkins & Rob Gregg, 5–15. Galloway, New Jersey: The Richard Stockton College of New Jersey.

Ferriss, L. 2018. "The Privilege of Language." *The Chronicle of Higher Education*, August 14, 2018. chronicle.com/blogs/linguafranca/2018/08/14/the-privilege-of-language/.

Hill, M. 2004. *After Whiteness: Unmaking an American Majority*. New York: New York University Press.

Johnson, S. 2019. "Colleges Lose a 'Stunning' 651 Foreign Language Programs in 3 Years." *The Chronicle of Higher Education*, January 22, 2019. chronicle.com/article/Colleges-Lose-a-Stunning-/245526.

Keenan, C. 2011. "20/20 Vision." In *Reaching 40. The Richard Stockton College of New Jersey*, edited by Ken Tompkins & Rob Gregg, 162–163. Galloway, New Jersey: The Richard Stockton College of New Jersey.

Kinsella, T. 2011. "Born (and Reborn) Within the Currents of Academia: The Shifting Literature Curriculum." In *Reaching 40. The Richard Stockton College of New Jersey*, edited by Ken Tompkins and Rob Gregg, 122–123. Galloway, New Jersey: The Richard Stockton College of New Jersey.

Looney, D., & Lusin, N. 2018. "Enrollments in Languages Other Than English in United States Institutions of Higher Education, Summer 2016 and Fall 2016: Preliminary Report." *Modern Language Association of America*. mla.org/content/download/83540/2197676/2016-Enrollments-Short-Report.pdf.

Morrison, T. 1992. *Playing in the Dark. Whiteness and the Literary Imagination*. Cambridge, Massachusetts: Harvard University Press.

Nelson, Linda Williamson. 2011. "Changing Lives: The Interdisciplinary Minors." In *Reaching 40. The Richard Stockton College of New Jersey*, edited by Ken Tompkins and Rob Gregg, 124–125 Galloway, New Jersey: The Richard Stockton College of New Jersey.

Porter, C. 2010. "Presidential Address 2009: English Is Not Enough." *Publications of the Modern Language Association of America*. bates.edu/french/files/2012/08/Porter_English-is-not-enough-PMLA-2010.pdf.

Pratt, M.L. 2003. "Building a New Public Idea about Language." *Profession* 34:3. mlajournals.org/doi/abs/10.1632/074069503X85472.

Prahlad, A. 2018. "Higher Education Year in Review." *Hanover Research*. New York: Hanover Research. hanoverresearch.com/reports-and-briefs/2018-year-in-review/.

Wyllie, J. 2018. "U.S. Foreign Language Enrollments Are Falling. Not at This University." *The Chronicle of Higher Education*, June 3, 2018. chronicle.com/article/US-Foreign-Language/243577.

SAFE ZONE

TANO RUBIO

My grandmother raised my father to speak what I came to learn through books, Spanish through a "forked tongue." [1] My large Hispanic family is for the most part multilingual, or at least his generation of it anyway. Chicano Spanish flows freely during our family visits, and it wasn't until I encountered social critic Gloria Anzaldúa that I learned how to embrace this interchange. In many of Anzaldúa's essays, she defends the often-overlooked cultural history of the American Southwest, and in her essay "How to Tame a Wild Tongue" she offers one of the most forthright ethnographies on this linguistic tradition. After encountering it in her essay, I soon came to realize that this tradition stems deep from mestizo roots entrenched in the American Southwest.

For the first six years of my life, I was surrounded by conversation that was fluid and hybrid. As a child, I wanted to speak Spanish, but in my house we spoke English mostly because my mother is a White woman from the Confederate South.

Spending my early years in New Mexico fostered a desire within me to speak Spanish so badly that I would walk around the house speaking my own iterations. Especially when I felt great waves of energy, I would burst forth in a mimicked glossolalia comprising all the immediate syllables on my tongue smashed together in quick succession, emphasizing my "rr's" and my "ñ's," with little success of expression, save for once. This time, when I was performing this ritual, I sputtered a word that my family ended up adopting as an interim word to use while searching for the term you

[1] "For those who are neither Spanish nor live in a country in which Spanish is the first language; for a people who live in a country in which English is the reigning tongue but who are not Anglo; for a people who cannot entirely identify with either standard (formal, Castilian) Spanish nor standard English, what recourse is left to them but to create their own language? A language which they can connect their identity to, one capable of communicating the realities and values true to themselves—a language with terms that are neither español ni inglés, but both. We speak a patois, a forked tongue, a variation of two languages." (Anzaldúa, G. 1987. *Borderlands: La Frontera*. San Francisco: Aunt Lute Books.)

actually mean. I will, for the first time in history, attempt to spell it with respect to English phonetics as I understand them: “whoa-tic-ka.”

It’s pronounced fast like this: whoaticka.

Here is an example of its usage:

You are reachin’ over the table for the mashed taters at Thanksgivin’. You pull the taters to you, and, as the casserole dish moves toward you, the servin’ spoon slips out and falls behind, smearin’ the nice Thanksgivin’ tablecloth your mother put out. Since you already have the taters in your hand, you motion toward your brother and ask, “Kyron, will you pass me the...the, umm…,” snapping your fingers, “...the whoaticka,” as you point to the spoon.

***

There is a phenomenon that has just happened to me that I’m sure has happened to you. If you have ever used any word-processing program, you are familiar with this occurrence. When typing a word that the program doesn’t recognize, there appears a squiggly red indicator that notifies you of its unrecognized properties. Now, if you are writing in the processor’s designated language and too lazy to decipher through the letters and find the mistakes and correct them yourself, you can right-click over the word, and it will appear with correct spelling. This tool is useful, especially for one as fleetingly minded as myself or my students.

In the previous section, the word I made up as a child, “whoaticka,” appears with this line slithering under it, stark against the overwhelming white and black of the document’s page. What’s odd is that I copied and pasted that word from another document that contained an earlier draft. In that document, I must have clicked the “Ignore all” function in the right-click menu because that squiggly line was not present anywhere in that draft. However, in this new document, that line is piously present as if it had never met this draft. The data don’t match, and my own forked tongue stands exposed in front of the rest of the page.

This word, made up by my childhood self and used in a contextual way around my family, will never be typed without me having to erase suspicion of its validity. I must rely on the process of each individual document’s “Ignore all” tolerant function to eradicate this word from scrutiny. There is no way that this word will be recognized, because it will not be used outside of this context, ever. It will also never be fully understood in its pronunciation except by those who know how I originally pronounced it.

Or perhaps you are more skilled than me at sounding out words.

You see, when I spelled it, I tried to represent it how I thought it could best be recognized. For example, I started it with the spelling "whoa-" because I wanted to emphasize the "wh-" sound at the beginning of the word. When I asked my spouse to spell whoaticka, a word she knew was sputtered in an attempt at "Spanish," she began to spell it with a "J," so it would read as "jor-."

She knows that Spanish words with the English "h-" sound begin with the letter "j," so she spelled it that way. However, if I were to stumble upon the word "jortica" with my Southern accent, I would thoughtlessly pronounce it with a "j" that sounded like the "j" in the word "jog," at first, only to remember it was Spanish, be embarrassed, revise my pronunciation, and continue reading.

In either spelling, the words "whoaticka" and "jortica" are scrutinized by the red squiggly line. I guess neither of us is correct. In accordance with my Southwestern American heritage, I must accept that I was never destined to speak correctly anyway.

***

As a high school English teacher, "speaking correctly" is what most might consider a prerequisite to the job. Speaking statistically, however, I am not a qualifying member of "most." [2]

I started teaching in 2015. Around that time, there was a growing national conversation sprouting around the term "safe spaces." This term, becoming quite controversial, had divisively infiltrated the field of education. If one were to Google the term "safe spaces," not only would its entry in Wikipedia be made readily available, but it would also become apparent that its usage has garnered enough traction to solidify its position in the Merriam–Webster Dictionary, defined as "a place (as on a college campus) intended to be free of bias, conflict, criticism, or potentially threatening actions, ideas, or conversations."

The origins of the term are rooted in a movement that sought to help victims of sexual assault recover from their trauma. The idea was to create spaces where people could come together and work through their own experiences with trauma in an environment that guaranteed the safety and

[2] I teach in a large school district in the Southeastern United States. According to the most recent data, my state has 975,222 students enrolled in its schools with 62,132 classroom teachers employed. My district has 43,830 of those students enrolled and 2,863 of those teachers employed. Of those numbers, my state has also reported only having 13 percent of its teachers being teachers of color, while having only 1 percent of its teachers identifying as Hispanic.

support of group therapy. The idea spread, however, to include people who had been affected by other forms of harassment, offering a sanctuary for those who are the consistent victims of systemic hegemony all throughout the sinews of the academic institution. Criticism arose when campus policies emerged that seemingly advocated for professors and other academic officials to start using "trigger warnings," which aimed to provide a heads-up for those who may feel aggressed by subject matter in the content that students were to encounter in the curriculum.

The criticism of "safe spaces" centers on the policies, and the broader implications thereof, that critics perceive as limiting one's right to free speech. Being prompted by policy to censor one's speech in the academic setting portended the abatement, to many academics, of one's right to govern one's own speech and, by extension, thoughts.

Unknowingly, when I entered this profession in August 2015, I was carrying some of the baggage of this national conversation with me. While there seemed to be some sense in wanting to create for students a space where they could feel "safe," I also, being a strong advocate for free speech, wanted to allow my students to experience the same liberties that are inherent in one's position in a democratic society. Being a first-year high school teacher, however, comes with its own initiatory set of issues itself, so being bogged down by the post-secondary controversy bombarding the issues of "safe spaces" took a back seat to all the other immediate demands that accompany the job. One of those demands being how to conduct oneself and one's class while being on lockdown, which is the primary scenario this essay attempts to capture.

The issue of "safe spaces" has largely consisted of conversations regarding post-secondary institutions. While there is certainly a validity to both sides of the debate—the overarching ideas that one can safeguard against aggression and that one ought to fight for one's right to free speech—both seem all too indulgent when one is faced with an immediate threat of violence. There is no protocol that can guide one correctly for how one might react when confronted with violence or even the impending threat. Simultaneously, I think there is a great void in this debate considering long-lasting and historical implications of race in this country, the brunt of which people of color must unnecessarily endure, that need to be addressed.

***

Prior to my first year of teaching high school English, there was a text that became a beacon, guiding me back, prodigal-like, into the institution from which I felt, for the greater part of my adolescence and young-adulthood, I had been effortlessly cast. Under the pressure of pervasive scrutiny, as a student, I faltered against the rules of language that demanded the concession of certain parts of my identity to its instruction. Toward the end of my high school career, I quit midyear in 11th grade, resigning never to return. Alas, I found myself returning nearly 10 years later, this time as a teacher.

Upon entering my graduate program of education, a time when millennial academics were green in the vast field of intellectual propagation, I flowered over this text. The aim of this text, which quickly became my mission as a new teacher, is to "broaden [an] understanding of literacy and literacy teaching and learning to include negotiating a multiplicity of discourses." [3]

Learning to "negotiate a multiplicity of discourses," however, does not come easily, as is evidenced by the controversy over the term "safe space." What I have learned throughout my time being a teacher, and also an academic, is that any form of negotiation requires something that many people are not willing to acquiesce: one's acceptance that they may not be right. I have also come to understand that a precedent to this acceptance is humiliation, and that is a cost that some are forced to reckon with more than others. However, it is a cost, nonetheless. Therefore, in order to hold space for any type of "multiplicity," this essay beseeches me to pay up.

***

My family moved to the suburbs of Nashville, Tennessee, when I was in kindergarten in an attempt to provide opportunities for my brother and me that would not have been so readily available to us in New Mexico. While my experiences in the Confederate South, and within its school systems in which I was transplanted, were less than ideal, I must admit that I had a more privileged upbringing than those in my extended family who were left behind in Albuquerque. I grew up in a community that prides itself on its good schools.

I recall being introduced to my class, midyear, as one envisions in a movie: The teacher calls the new student in front of the class for introduction and assimilation. Vivid accuracy of memory evades me, but the feeling rests in my gut as bitter sediment. I turned to my teacher and began crying. I remember being asked what had prompted my discomfort and conjuring the reply, "They were all looking at me."

---

[3] Cazden, Courtney; Cope, Bill; Fairclough, Norman; Gee, Jim; et al. 1996. "Pedagogy of Multiliteracies: Designing Social Futures." *Harvard Educational Review* 66(1): 60.

As a young elementary school boy who had recently moved from New Mexico to Tennessee, I found it extraordinarily hard differentiating New Mexico from Mexico and Hispanic from Mexican. My defenses:

"No. I am not from Mexico. I am from NEW Mexico. It's a state too!"
"No. I am HISPANIC. I was not born in Mexico."

Eventually I learned to answer the question of my origin with my city of birth: Huntsville, Alabama.

***

The goal of a pedagogy of multiliteracies is twofold, but I'm going to focus on one: the attempt "to extend the idea and scope of literacy pedagogy to account for the context of our culturally and linguistically diverse and increasingly globalized societies, for the multifarious cultures that interrelate and the plurality of texts that circulate" within the classroom.[4] In theory, this pedagogical approach illuminates the path toward a progressive, democratic society—a society I, as a green teacher, thought my country was working toward. A society in which I felt, in my early twenties, the only meaningful contribution I could offer was my employment as one of its architects.

Since reading "A Pedagogy of Multiliteracies," one word has haunted my teaching practice, every so often stirring that bitter sediment that remains in my gut. The New London Group exhorts that only by "dealing authentically" with differences in the classroom "can we create out of diversity and history a new, vigorous, and equitable public realm."[5] This word "authentic" strips the pretense from any methodology I was or have been presented with as an English teacher. It is hard to tell someone to get in front of a room of teenagers and tell them to act "authentic," especially if you are to win their respect. Teaching is often prescribed. As teachers, we are exposed to strategies and methods that ensure student success and learning, none of which easily lends itself to authenticity. When I encountered this word in an academic text on pedagogy, I was struck with its audacious vulnerability and its inherent messiness. What did "authentic" mean for the classroom? How does one conjure authenticity?

---

[4] Cazden, Courtney; Cope, Bill; Fairclough, Norman; Gee, Jim; et al. 1996. "Pedagogy of Multiliteracies: Designing Social Futures." *Harvard Educational Review* 66(1): 61.

[5] Ibid, 69.

When I think of what I experience when I am in many classrooms as a student, and even when I attend professional development as a teacher, every time I am asked to describe what a classroom is supposed to look like, I struggle to convey a concrete authenticity. The only way I know if something is authentic is if I feel it. Feelings aren't quantifiable. The moment I try to capture it, as disarming as the concept aims to be, the word "authentic," all at once, becomes inaccessible.

Not three months into my master's program in education, I was offered a position at my district's alternative high school. Having very limited knowledge of what constituted alternative education, and even more limited experience, I took the job.

***

A couple of months in, the school had a "Yellow" lockdown, which I came to understand later as a soft lockdown. "Soft" meaning not as scary of a lockdown as a real lockdown—a "Code Red"—but a lockdown, nonetheless. Being on a "Code Yellow" means classes are to continue as usual, but doors remain closed and students are to stay in the room until further notified. It is a bit exhausting because even though you are just as curious as the students as to what caused the lockdown, you have to pretend that things are normal and continue class. Or so says the protocol.

Unfortunately, no one had reviewed the lockdown procedures with me during the first few weeks of my employment. So when they came over the intercom to announce the "Code Yellow," I scampered through the room, cussing not-so-under my breath, searching for the list of lockdown procedures, which I knew had to be somewhere in my employee handbook. By the time I had figured out the protocol, the "Code Yellow" was called off, and the assistant principal, Ms. Rogers, came into my class and assured everyone that everything was okay. I'm sure the need for assurance was apparent when she saw my face, which must have shown an awkward bewilderment.

The following semester, we had another "Code Yellow," this time for a lot longer. As soon as we had received the all clear, it seemed the whole school flooded into the bathroom. As I peed, the stream muffled the boys' noise. My built-up tension waned as the splash harshened, a comforting solo amidst a chorus of chaos. The stall offered shelter, a relief. Almost as immediately as it was realized, my solitude was interrupted by an alarming announcement over the intercom: "CODE RED! CODE RED!"

Ms. Woods, the team lead-teacher, yelled into the bathroom, "Come on! Let's go! Go to my room! Get out!"

I couldn't see her, but I zipped my pants and opened the stall door. *Is it bad that I am stopping to wash my hands?* I thought before turning off the faucet and running toward the door. She was pulling the boys out of the bathroom, shoving them in the direction of her classroom, "Let's go! Let's go!"

When I got out of the bathroom, two other teachers were yelling at the last two students in the hallway, whom I began guiding into my classroom. As I closed the door, I turned to the wall on which the protocol was taped and checked to see if I was following it.

Lights off. Check. Blinds down. Check. Door locked. Check, I thought. I walked over to the door. Check. Email list of students, first and last name, in room to the front office. I pulled out my phone. Check. Make sure all students are sitting in the pre-designated "Safe Zone." I looked at the chart hanging on the wall, "What classroom number is this?"

"You don't know your classroom number?" Tavion responded accusingly, which was fair.

"Never mind." All the "Safe Zones" were conveniently in the same spot in each room. I commanded, "Go over to that table over there," pointing the pair over to one, which was, if I read the chart correctly, in the "Safe Zone."

"Why?!" They both questioned, even though they both got up and moved.

"Just do," I turned around, "okay." Check, I hoped.

***

Growing up, nurtured mostly by White women, I naturally felt inspired by, and almost eerily akin to, narratives portrayed in movies like *Freedom Writers* and *The Blind Side*. As I watched these types of movies, gazing from the comfort of my own home prior to teaching, their portrayals touched my heart.

However, the empathy evoked by these movies is too often prescribed and, especially within the academic institution, used as motivation for many new teachers who get thrown into situations for which they soon come to realize they are underprepared. As a middle-class society, we stand, as Sesshu Foster critiques in his poetic essay, as tourists, who flee during the off season, connecting to principles of redemption and promise as if walking through an exhibit in a carefully curated museum.[6]

I was often confronted by the artifice of class tourism when I started teaching. Returning to the front of the class as a teacher of the economic and

[6] Foster, Sesshu. 2018. *City of the Future*. Los Angeles: Kaya Press.

racial demographics I teach, I joined the display before the often-saccharine gawks from the same women who raised me. When made aware of my returning to the field of education, they appeared assuaged, proud, hands crossed heart, beaming with praise:

"That must be really rewarding."

"They need good teachers."

"Wow, good for you."

Gloria Ladson–Billings, in her essay "Preparing Teachers for Diverse Student Populations: A Critical Race Theory Perspective," uncovers hidden biases that are ingrained in the training of pre-service teachers in the United States. Ladson–Billings discusses how students of color became targeted through federal, as well as local, programming. Programming, brought about by the 1983 landmark educational report, "A Nation at Risk," that inevitably led to the association of students of color with the term "at-risk." "A Nation at Risk" was a national education survey that concluded that the American academic institution was at severe risk of failing in a competitive world market.

In the many years following this report, the academic institution has set forth myriad programming to address this apparent risk, which has led to severe educational reform that is ongoing nearly fifty years later. While there are many avenues for one to follow regarding the exposure of educational schisms brought about by this report and subsequent reformation, Ladson–Billings focuses on the growing need for reformation in educational preparation programs. She has noted the glaring, and foreseeably unachievable, responsibility facing these programs in educating teachers-to-be and their responsibility to the diverse demands of teaching students, particularly students of color: "Typical teacher education students have led monocultural, ethnically encapsulated lives that have not afforded them the opportunities to broaden their linguistic and communicative repertoires. It is unlikely that a university-based course will adequately prepare teachers to achieve this communicative facility."

Research has noted the high turnover rate in schools with "at-risk" populations, and, as evidenced by the racial demographics of my state's school systems, many of the teachers in the profession could not have had the same experience at "negotiating a multiplicity of discourses" simply due to the lack of multiplicity in the educational field. The field, like many professional fields, is overwhelmingly White, which contributes to an overall majority of professionals entering a field in which they themselves are experientially bereft, which brings into question professional qualification.

***

"You scared, Mr. Rubio." Tavion mocked. I saw his eyes reading my face. A familiar, yet subdued, adrenaline glossed his eyes. His neck cocked, supporting what seemed to be a slight grin at my discomfort.

"No, I'm not scared. I just don't know what the 'Code Red' is for, so we are just going to sit here and wait it out."

He responded, "What's goin' on?"

"I don't know, Tay, but we just have to stay right here until we hear differently."

"Who? Someone come in here shootin', I'm goin' out that door." Kimora finally chimed in. Up until this point, she had been anxiously quiet. *And I'll be right behind you*, I thought as I straightened my posture to muster some confidence.

"That's not gonna happen, Kimora. No one's gonna come shootin' up the school."

"You scared, Mr. Rubio," muttered Tavion, nodding his head, still looking at my face. This time, I couldn't tell if he was asking or telling me. "Shiiit, let me go home and get some stuff, we'll be a'ight."

"Tay, we're just gonna stay here for now." I said, asserting a feigned confidence. I was trying to convince him, but he knew I wasn't convinced myself. I couldn't tell if I was scared or not. My heart had settled, but the adrenaline clenched my fists, which were now white to keep from shaking. I released the strain and took a deep breath.

Tavion tried to fill the silence, "I'm goin', they come in here."

I believed him and decided I wouldn't stop him.

He continued, "I ain't dyin' at school. Let me call my homies, we'll be a'ight. Lemme use your phone, Mr. Rubio."

"No, Tay, you're not gonna call your homies to come help shoot up who's shootin' up the school. That's not even gonna happen, anyway. I don't know what's going on, but we'll be fine."

"When we gonna know?" Kimora's gaze was begging for something from mine. She wanted the comfort of certainty, which was a luxury I couldn't afford in my inexperience.

"I don't know." I offered what I could as I looked into her eyes, returning her gaze.

The first time I met Kimora, she entered my classroom and sat at the nearest table awaiting my instruction. Carl, crazy and nappy dreaded, lost all sense over her in my class. After I separated them in my seating arrangement, Carl looked at me, and said "I see what you're doing, Mr. Rubio. Why don't you want me to sit by my boo?"

I ignored the question and kept eyes on Kimora, who snapped at him to shut up. Her movements caught my attention. Without compromising her tight composure, she sat straight up. The tightness of her composure intrigued me.

She was a "transitional student," meaning she was moving from the juvenile detention center back into the public-school system. Her maroon, thick-rimmed glasses covered her eyes so that I couldn't see into them from any other perspective other than when her eyes met mine. She had to allow me to see them.

I exhaled slowly through my nose to calm my heart rate. "We're gonna be alright, Kiki," I offered. And this time, we all bought it.

They turned and talked to one another, leaving me to unravel the anxiety swirling around my thoughts.

***

Researchers have found that there exists a common defining feature of alternative high schools. Alternative learning settings, as they are often referred to in the research, are typically serving students who are labeled as "disenfranchised." These "disenfranchised" students have not or do not align with the status quo within a more traditional educational setting.

Alternative schools have more popularly come to be known as places for students who are at risk of failing in a regular education system. Students enrolled in these schools not only are academically at risk, but also have a higher proclivity to health-risk behavior as well, including but not limited to behaviors involving drug use, diet, physical and sexual activity, and mental health. More often than not, these students are a racial minority or of lower socioeconomic status.

***

"Where you stay at?" Tavion asked Kimora.

"Out in the Eastside."

"Oh, forreal? I ain't know you stay over there? Whatchu do over there?"

"I just stay in my room, and listen to music, and," she hesitantly looks at me, "smoke."

"Ohh, what's your number? Maybe I can come up there 'n put the gas in you."

My ears perked up and I snapped out of my thoughts. "Tavion, don't try to sell weed right in front of me," I said, with a slight eye roll.

"I ain't sellin', Mr. Rubio. I ain't even sell weed no more."

"Yes, you are. You just said you wanted to 'put the gas in her.' I'm not slow. I know what you mean." They both started laughing. "What? I know what 'gas' is, and you said you wanted to 'put it in her.'"

"That's not what that means," defended Kimora.

"Then what does it mean?"

"It means I wanna put the gas in her," answered Tavion. They looked at each other and giggled.

"Doesn't that mean you want to sell weed to her?"

"No," Tavion motioned toward Kimora, "it mean I wanna put it in her."

"I don't get it. That sounds like you want to sell her weed." I didn't want to say what it actually sounded like.

"No," he clarified, "I wanna go put it in her."

"So, what, you want to, like, smoke weed together or something?"

"Yeeeeeessssss," they said in unison, Kimora annoyedly and Tavion mischievously.

"Oh, okay. Then why didn't you just say that?" We all smirked at this point, thankful for the diversion. "Well, okay then. Why do you guys have to talk about that right now?"

"Whatch'you mean?" asked Kimora.

"Like, why don't you guys ever talk about anything different?"

"Whatch'you mean?"

"I feel like all y'all wanna talk about its weed, violence, gangs, shooting, whatever or nothing."

"What do you mean, y'all?"

"I'm sorry, Kiki, I don't mean you, but, like, y'all were just talking about it in front of me."

"Because, what else are we gonna talk about? That's pretty much all I do."

"Yeahhh. But don't you want to like get, um, learn to talk about other things?"

"Like what?"

"I don't know, like, umm, I don't know, but there is more to life than weed and stuff." I tried to shuffle through my brain, but because of the ever-looming presence of being under a "Red" lockdown, I couldn't focus enough to offer a valid suggestion.

"Like what?"

"I don't know. But there will be. Later in your life." I thought that would suffice.

"But what else can I talk about other than my life?" Tavion chimed in.

"But there's more to you than guns and gangs and weed."

"Like what?"

"Okay, stop saying that, Kimora." I turned to Tavion, "I know that you know that there is."

He broke our gaze to look beyond me, "But you don't understand."

"I know. Y'all say that all the time, but, like, I do understand, just, like, um, okay, so when you're young, I mean we're all three young, but y'all are younger than me." I paused to collect my thoughts. "As you get older, you see everything, and then, like, you see a little bit more outside of that. Does that make sense? I feel like you say I don't understand, but I at least understand something."

"But, y'all don't get what it's like for us. On the streets."

What do you mean, "y'all"?! My mind turned defensive, but I couldn't come up with any retort that would validate her experience, while also upholding my own authority. "That may be true, but I understand something outside of that, that's, um, equally as true."

"Y'all really don't." Our eyes were challenging each other now. But our gaze remained unbroken.

"But don't you want to get out of the streets?"

"Oh, I am. I'm goin' to college, and gonna get out. And I'mma get my granny out too."

I felt the stalemate rapidly approaching, and I didn't want to leave this conversation in conflict, nor did I want to make their experience seem invalid. I realized the resolve wasn't theirs or mine to offer. "I mean. I just think there is more to life than, like, that life."

"Not for me." Tay asserts his eyes into my line of sight—brown on brown. "This is my life. You just don't understand."

"No. I don't. But, like, I get it."

***

Throughout the writing of this narrative, I realized I had entered into the teaching profession never expecting my high school students to have a firm grasp on the complexities of race relations in this country. In fact, I entered it without one myself. To say that they do is a vast oversimplification, but there is room for growth where I had previously not entertained. There is very little direction in any standard curriculum model that I have come across that helps teachers better prepare for this conversation. Even in situations outside the classroom, there is still a lot of ground to be covered.

This conversation with Tavion and Kimora has always fascinated me, even more so considering the circumstances surrounding its inception.[7]

Everyone has moments where they wish they could go back and respond in situations that were less than ideal with a more ideal response that represents them in a better light. I believe this is somewhat of a universal experience. That is the purpose of reflection. In the spirit of authenticity, I am attempting to recapture this experience with as much accuracy as possible because I want to provide space for the multiplicity represented. However, there is a direction I wish I could have taken the conversation had I been afforded the time.

bell hooks, in her dialogue with Ron Scapp entitled "Building a Teaching Community," instructs that we "have been compelled to return to the body to speak about ourselves as subjects in history. We are all subjects in history. We must return ourselves to a state of embodiment in order to deconstruct the way power has been traditionally orchestrated in the classroom, denying subjectivity to some groups and according it to others."[8] Because learning, especially in high school, takes place in the mind, people often forget that there is a physical responsibility to teaching as well. When I stand in front of my students, I am doing so in my body, in my flesh. Language, as an extension of the mind, and therefore the body, presents itself in a physical way as well. When both the body and language function in the world, they are doing so as entities that contain more within themselves than meets the eye.

***

Kyron is my brother. His skin color takes after my mother's, who is from Alabama. Roberto is my father. His skin color reflects his heritage. When we were younger, I was compared to my father. Kyron, to my mother. Now, I think if you look at the length of my legs and my high cheekbones, my stature and face resemble my mother's. And if you look at my brother's hands, well, let's just say he definitely has the arthritic gene plaguing my father's family. Sorry, Kyron.

---

[7] In the book *Why Are All the Black Kids Still Sitting Together in the Cafeteria?*, writer Beverly Daniel Tatum summarizes a study done by Claremont Graduate University researchers who "concluded that the disparity in media coverage [of police brutality against minority races other than Black] highlights the fact that issues of racial discrimination in the United States are typically framed in terms of Black–White race relations, while the experiences of other groups of color are overlooked."

[8] hooks, bell. 1994. *Teaching to Transgress*. New York: Routledge.

But still, I resemble my father.

When my family first moved back to the Confederate South, we moved from a majority-Hispanic community to a majority-White one. My mother's family replaced my father's, and I began to be socialized in a society that views things as Black and White while inhabiting the White section of that society. My grandfather on my mother's side owned and operated a tile-laying company. Being in the construction workforce for so many years in the Confederate South had caused him to come in contact with people who were consistently referred to as "Roberto's people." As I grew, my cultural heritage of being Hispanic became tainted more and more with that label. I wanted to disassociate myself with it so much that, when I was in college, I decided to study French instead of Spanish as to better fulfill my academic pursuits as an English student. My father was appalled and blamed me for abandoning my heritage. I blamed him for neglecting to teach me Spanish when I was a child. There was no sense that either of us had anyone to blame but the other, and yet there continued a gnawing sensation for me that he was right.

***

Later in the school year, Tavion ended up getting suspended for the remainder of that year. He received a discipline referral (one of many) from another teacher. Outside the school, waiting for his ride, he looked at me as he unfolded his suspension papers.

Frustrated, he held the papers in front of him confounded, "What?! What does this mean? What is this?"

I held out my hand, offering to translate the description of his offenses. It said something about how he was making drug references in class.

He hurried me. "What does it mean?"

"I don't know Tay. I wasn't there, but it says you're suspended for the rest of the year. You can't come back. You can bring your mom or someone back to the principal and they can talk with him and he can…"

"My mom? My mom in the hospital!" And he turned away.

This assertion silenced me. Perhaps I could have interceded on his behalf, but as a first-year teacher, I was unaware of the procedure of such an intercession. The one who had written the referral(s) had been teaching longer than Tavion and my ages combined. I was in no position to dispute. Or so I thought. At that time, I couldn't make sense of the feelings stirring in my gut. A feeling I have since found a language for but have been frustrated at my ignorant silence in the past, a feeling Tavion thought I could never understand.

At that moment, one of Tavion's female cousins came out of the school and told him that some boy had been picking on her and that he should kick his ass. She pointed him across the parking lot where the boy stood. Tavion took off.

Ms. Woods, who had been standing next to me, witnessing my interchange with Tavion, grabbed me by the arm and said, "Go get him."

Tavion, in anger-induced tunnel vision, was storming across the parking lot when his aunt's car intercepted him. "Tavion, get in the car! Get in the car!"

"Tavion, listen to her," Ms. Woods and I encouraged.

His aunt parked the car and got out. "Tavion, get in the car!"

Her eyes turned toward the school resource officer, whose countenance was now fixed upon Tavion. Ms. Woods and I grabbed Tavion and started pushing him into the car. His aunt became emphatic.

"Tay, look at your skin. They don't care about you! Get in the car!"

"No, ma'am. We aren't all like that," Ms. Woods responded, now blocking Tavion in between the passenger door and the side of the car. She was speaking as a representative on behalf of herself, first and foremost, and others like her. Like Tavion. Like me.

"Tavion, baby, go on. Get in the car."

Tavion's head ducked into the passenger's seat. I stood back, astounded at what had just occurred, somewhat cinematically, something that, to me, appeared inexplicable, in which now I had been recruited as an unwitting participant.

***

Tavion, Kimora, and I heard jingling keys penetrating the doorknob lock.

"We're good! 'Code Red's' over. Good job, y'all." Ms. Rogers, the assistant principal, turned my room's lights back on and surveyed the room. She looked at us three, sitting at the back table. I could tell she was judging our location in the classroom. We were in the wrong spot.

As we adjusted to the light, I glanced back at the wall that held the lockdown procedures and the "Safe Zone" chart on which I had earlier relied. I thought we had found our "Safe Zone," but I misread the chart.

***

To say that there is a definite spot where one can be considered "safe" while under a lockdown is based on the relevance of what one considers safety. Safety can never really be guaranteed. If the situation calls for it, we are instructed as teachers to make a judgement call as to whether the class is to leave the classroom. The call for action is determined by the location of the threat.

The situation that called for the "Code Red" in this essay was connected to a shooting that had taken place across town. At the time of the "Code Yellow," the suspect was seen driving in the direction of the school. The school went under a "Code Red" when the suspect had turned onto the same road as the school. Unbeknownst to anyone at the time, the suspect had been in our school building earlier that day attempting to pick up another student at the school prior to the shooting. Because the suspect was not approved on the student's profile for pickup, the ladies in the front office had turned him away without our student.

I can't say whether knowing this information makes me feel any safer. Someone who could have easily been involved in that shooting, had the front office clerk allowed him to leave, was amidst those of us under lockdown. Because neither he nor anyone else knew that the shooting was in some way connected to him, he did not pose a threat during the lockdown.

I did not come to know any of this information until months later when it was rumored through the teachers in passing conversation around the lunch table. Often as teachers at the alternative high school we are subject to many scenarios that would cause one to question the legitimacy of any type of protocol. Being considered alternative immediately removes what we do from the mainstream, which is what protocol attempts to corral. To say that I understand what constitutes proper protocol for safety is a bit of a stretch, but I must admit I have an intimate understanding of the relative nature of "safe."

***

The controversy over the phrase "safe space" hints not at our lack of understanding of the need for safety. When it comes down to it, people are going to seek safety no matter what the dilemma. Safety is not a matter of freedom; it's a matter of necessity. Rather the controversy exposes our inexperience with authenticity, which requires vulnerability.

It was the vulnerability of this scenario that helped me build a relationship with Tavion and Kimora outside the pressures of the classroom. Having more protocol surrounding these issues wouldn't have eliminated the threat. I'm not sure of the effect of this experience on these two students, but I know for me it was transformative. To some extent, it was my lack of understanding of protocol that provided space for growth and understanding.

We need more conversation that addresses the issues preceding the need for safety, such as race and class disenfranchisement. For many people of color in this nation, there is a great need for safety, but there are very few areas where we can find it, and often when it appears that we have found our safe zones, something shifts and stirs our unease once again. The lights come on, and judgment glares at us once again. James Baldwin, in conversation with the celebrity anthropologist Margaret Mead entitled *A Rap on Race*, asserts "if one is going to change history—and we have to change history—we have to change ourselves because we are history." This sentiment from 1970 is rapidly approaching fifty years of age, and yet the truth behind it remains vibrant throughout each new generational shift. I cannot offer a sense of safety within this essay because I am struggling to find it myself on a daily basis. Gloria Anzaldúa ends her essay "How to Tame a Wild Tongue" with the line "Stubborn, persevering, impenetrable as stone, yet possessing a malleability that renders us unbreakable, we the mestizas and mestizos, will remain." I believe this for the simple fact that what you are reading has come out of this urgent need to remain.

To remain in the past, to remain in the present, to remain in the future, for myself and the people like me, is to remain safe.

Sources

Anzaldúa, G. 1987. *Borderlands: La Frontera*. San Francisco: Aunt Lute Books.

Baldwin, J., & Mead, M. 1971. *A Rap on Race*. New York: J. B. Lippincott Company.

Beken, J.A., Williams, J., Combs, J.P., & Slate, J.R. 2009. "At-Risk Students at Traditional and Academic Alternative School Settings: Differences in Math and English Performance Indicators." *Florida Journal of Educational Administration & Policy*, 3(1), 49–61.

Cazden, C., Cope, B., Fairclough, N., Gee, J., Kalantzis, M., Kress, G., Luke, A., Luke, C., Michaels, S., & Nakata, M. 1996. "Pedagogy of Multiliteracies: Designing Social Futures." *Harvard Educational Review* 66(1), 60-92. newarcproject.pbworks.com/f/Pedagogy+of+Multiliteracies_New+London+Group.pdf.

Foster, S. 2018. *City of the Future*. Los Angeles: Kaya Press.

Grunbaum, J.A., Kann, L., Kinchen, S.A., Ross, J.G., Gowda, V.R., Collins, J.L., & Kolbe, L.J. 2000. "Youth Risk Behavior Surveillance: National Alternative High School Youth Risk Behavior Survey, United States, 1998." *Journal of School Health,* 70(1), 5–17.

Guin, K. 2004. "Chronic Teacher Turnover in Urban Elementary Schools." *Education Policy Analysis Archives*, 12(42). epaa.asu.edu/epaa/v12n42/.

hooks, b. 1994. *Teaching to Transgress*. New York: Routledge.

Ingersoll, R. 2001. "Teacher Turnover and Teacher Shortages: An Organizational Analysis." repository.upenn.edu/gse_pubs/94.

Johnson, K.E., & Taliaferro, L.A. 2012. "Health Behaviors and Mental Health of Students Attending Alternative High Schools: A Review of the Research Literature." *Journal for Specialists in Pediatric Nursing*. 17(2), 79–97.

Ladson–Billings, G.J. 1999. "Preparing Teachers for Diverse Student Populations: A Critical Race Theory Perspective." *Review of Research in Education*. 24, 211–247.

Lehr, C.A., Tan, C.S., & Ysseldyke, J. 2009. "Alternative Schools: A Synthesis of State-Level Policy and Research." *Remedial and Special Education*. 30(1), 19–32.

Lukianoff, G. & Haidt, J. 2015. "The Coddling of the American Mind." *The Atlantic*, September 2015. theatlantic.com/magazine/archive/2015/09/the-coddling-of-the-american-mind/399356/#Cognitive%20Disorders.

May, H.E., & Copeland, E.P. 1998. "Academic Persistence and Alternative High Schools: Student and Site Characteristics." *The High School JournalI.* 81(4), 199–208.

Tatum, B.D. 2017. *Why Are All the Black Kids Sitting Together in the Cafeteria? And Other Conversations About Race*. New York: Basic Books.

Waldman, K. 2016. "The Trapdoor of Trigger Words." *Slate*, September 5, 2016. slate.com/articles/double_x/cover_story/2016/09/what_science_can_tell_us_about_trigger_warnings.html.

LET'S TALK ABOUT IT: WHITE DISCRIMINATION AN ACT OF DOMESTIC TERRORISM

LUCÍA GALLENO VILLAFÁN

At 23, I came to the United States from Peru to find work. I got a job as a waitress first, but I had not come for that. A few months later, I enrolled in a secretarial school in California. As soon as I graduated, I looked for jobs in the newspaper and called many businesses. The U.S. culture looked so extraordinary to me. There were so many Christian churches and preachers sending blessings I assumed Americans would be kind to me. Yet people hung up on me when they heard my accent. They had no patience. Eventually, I called an immigration attorney looking for a bilingual secretary, interpreter and translator. By then, my conversational English was stronger, though my accent remained strong. However, this time the employer was interested in interviewing me. With a wife from Colombia, he understood my accented English. I got the job working with various attorneys and learned about legal procedures, particularly regarding immigration.

My interpreting took me to Universal Studios to work for the International Sales Division in Latin America with Vice President of Sales Francisco Padilla. Paco, as he asked to be called, had transferred from Mexico City after the big 1985 earthquake. This job provided me an opportunity to build interpersonal relationships with all kinds of Americans and foreigners. In this environment, discrimination was taken seriously. People were educated to avoid it, yet that wasn't enough all of the time. Sometimes it did not happen as desired. An African American secretary verbally harassed by her boss warned him to change his attitude or she would file a complaint. She spoke loudly and firmly asking for respect. The boss ultimately toned down his pushy and discriminatory style because there was a system in place to sanction him. Witnessing their confrontation made me think equality might be available to me too. It was real and possible to expect to be treated equal. That is the law. This gave me a big boost.

I believed times were changing with respect to race, sex and creed. However, I continued to encounter other occasions of discrimination. The confusion surrounding the HIV epidemic led to discrimination against those presumed infected. This was when gay men were dying quickly, and no treatment effectively combatted the disease. Understanding was limited, and fear was the most common response even among the well-informed. Some executives at Universal Studios became thinner and paler until news arrived that they had been hospitalized, and then their passing was reported. The chain of deaths made people wonder when Vice President Francisco Padilla was going to show symptoms. Many thought my boss was gay. This meant Paco's entire environment, which included me, was dangerous. People avoided us and sent their secretaries to deliver messages and requests to me. This discriminatory behavior saddened me, but it did relieve me from dealing with their false civility. Paco did not say much, but his was an angry silence. The HIV epidemic brought to the surface the latent discrimination controlled in normal circumstances. Paco was a lawyer over 60 and single. The youngest of his family, he took good care of himself. He came from a well-off, traditional, urban Mexican family. As is true of many immigrants, Paco needed friends and felt isolated and detached from the excitement and friendliness of his Mexican culture. Yet people at work did not care about his needs for affiliation and inclusion. They made him the target of their jokes putting down immigrants. When his millionaire uncle died, Paco quit and went back to Mexico. He was finally able to let everybody know who he was and tell them to shove it.

His office closed, and I became unemployed. I had learned that fearful minds with harmful intentions will always find ways to discriminate. I decided to return home to Peru to finish my studies while I waited for my resident card.

Discovering Rural America in Arkansas

At 33, after waiting a decade, my son and I received our green cards and returned to the U.S. I would follow the academic path. This was my way out from the political turmoil that was striking Peru—terrorism and state terror. With the additional knowledge acquired through my studies, and my previous exposure to West Coast culture, I thought I understood American dynamics. Studying Romance languages and literature with a designated emphasis in film at the University of California, Berkeley, life looked progressive. I saw an institutional system fostering equality, support and creativity. Then, after completing my Ph.D., I began my first position in

2002 as an assistant Spanish professor in Russellville, Arkansas, at Arkansas Tech University.

My conception and understanding of rural America differed vastly from reality. Once in Russellville, I felt I had traveled back in time. White people were puzzled that a Hispanic woman could speak English let alone be a professor at the local institution. This demonstrated limited perceptions of the potentiality of Hispanics. One English professor, from the Deep South, often looked down on me and cracked jokes about my accent. Other White colleagues who had little experience with other international people and cultures found me exotic—a word that denotes so many things—but would not develop a friendship. They could address me as an academic "other," a subject of academic research if they were studying Latin American cultures, but beyond that they had no true interest in knowing me. One former alumna from Duke University, who worked also as an English professor at Arkansas Tech, tried to help. She encouraged me to leave this region because I would have a hard time flourishing. She told me, the racist and traditional mentality of this area does not match with your *hispanidad*. She had tried to leave earlier in her career but had not been able to find an alternate position.

A few weeks later, I experienced more of the racism in Arkansas. One day on an outing with a Latin American colleague, I approached a store cashier to pay for a silk shirt. The White cashier examined the shirt and looked at me. I felt her questioning my ability to buy something so pretty and pricy with her interrogative eyes and funny twitching gestures. The memory of the young Black American who expected respect from her boss served as a model for me in these types of moments. Memories of my mother taking my brothers and me to see the film *Uncle Tom*, my readings of the history of the Black Panthers, documentaries about African Americans being lynched and the work of Dr. Martin Luther King Jr. all traveled through my mind, reminding me how discrimination has come to be engrained in some regions. Ultimately, the discrimination in this store and at work elicited a sense of compassion in me. Their world was the size of a bean. Most of them had not exposed themselves to other cultures even within their own large country.

I could have stayed in Arkansas. The landscape of Central Arkansas offered summer sonatas made by orchestras of crickets at night, and fall greeted winter with dancing and falling leaves, but the dominant discriminatory mentality of colleagues was too much. I applied to other jobs in academia and soon moved to Shelby, North Carolina, believing that it was more advanced.

Speaking Up in North Carolina

My job as an assistant Spanish professor at the local university was going fine until the department chair went on sabbatical. The permanent and interim chairs had a history of disagreement and divergent visions for the future of the department. I found myself in the middle of this boxing match. It was an unhealthy environment, yet I had to continue working there. I was trapped by my responsibilities as a single mom. I had bought a little house with the hope that my son would join me.

In my new position, I was also coordinator of the international teaching assistants. During the spring break, one of the TAs checked out a school laptop with her to the beach. Three TAs took pictures of themselves at the beach and transferred the files to the computer to send to their families abroad. After that, the TA deleted the pictures and returned the laptop to the library. Unfortunately, they forgot to remove the pictures from the deleted folder and the librarian found them. The librarian at this Christian–Baptist university accused the TAs of misusing library resources. The permanent chair sent an email to the faculty accusing the Latin American TAs of pornographic behavior. I contacted the TAs to hear their stories regarding the pictures. They brought the pictures to my office. The pictures were of young women in bikinis and showed less flesh than the blond students in bikinis sunbathing by the university's pond. What was really the problem?

I suggested the TAs contact the chair to clear up any misunderstanding before they returned home. They did and reported that he said that everything was all right. Later, at a departmental meeting, I addressed this matter, suggesting we implement a protocol for investigation instead of only accepting one person's interpretation or hearsay. This angered the chair. How could a Latina voice that she expected fairness for the TAs from Latin America? How could I not keep quiet as a submissive subhuman living in segregated North Carolina? He set in motion a number of decisions that would lead to the university not renewing my contract. That was my sixth year as an assistant professor. The personnel committee found his claims unfounded. Yet, with the support of the new dean, the chair did not issue my contract. The chair had befriended the new dean, who was later removed from his position after becoming involved with a student. This rampant discrimination articulated collaboration among good old boys. They wanted me to disappear, but I wanted to remain in town at my house. The president of the institution offered me money, provided I did not file a report with the Equal Employment Opportunity Commission in Charlotte. I filed the report because equality and fair treatment is the least a human can expect, especially at a Christian institution.

Unemployed, with a mortgage, and living through the economic crisis, I did not repent. Instead, I looked for new jobs. This was a dead end because the chair would choose the perfect words so nobody would hire me. (This was reported to me by one of the interviewers). Though colleagues spoke on my behalf and stated that the department was dysfunctional, the interviewers were not willing to take the risk of hiring me.

My mother asked if it had been worth it to request fairness and fight for those young women. My mother, who believed in women's rights and social justice, was questioning this when her daughter paid a high price. She would let go of anything if she could free me from suffering. In contrast, my father, who has been involved in politics, gave me his kind support. He understood that there are ideas one must act upon regardless of the price. Yet I did ask myself: Could I fit in this segregated, discriminatory community and also be able to deal with misogynists? Was there space for me, a Latinoamericana?

At last, I received a visiting professor position at Furman University in South Carolina for a year. I spent an average of $400 a week driving back and forth and had just enough left to pay the mortgage and buy food.

Showing My Identity

While working at Furman, a professor told me his colleague from Queens University of Charlotte, North Carolina, was looking for a visiting Spanish professor for a yearlong contract. I applied and interviewed but was not selected. The committee opted for a Spaniard candidate. Yet, when they realized that she could not be hired because she lacked the legal papers, I was offered the position. Later on, a tenure-track position opened up. There was a national search, and I succeeded in earning the job. Since 2008, I have been working at Queens.

In North Carolina, at the university and in other locations, people often ignored my Hispanic name and instead switched the pronunciation to the Italian way. I used to go along with this as an act of courtesy and to avoid dealing with their tiresome White discrimination against Hispanics. This behavior, however, meant submitting. It was easy to do. Finally, after listening to their repetitive Italianizing assumptions, I realized that people did not want to listen to the sound of my Spanish name. I needed to move from requesting fairness and equal treatment to integrating my *hispanidad* into the host culture to become American and Latina. I began stating my name with more Spanish clarity and spelling it out while looking directly into people's eyes. Were American listeners able to transcend discomfort? Unless people let me know they got it, I began spelling out my saintly name. This was a bridge that I created verbally to connect with all Americans culturally so that together we could transcend each other's assumptions. It is the same for me when I hear Kathleen, Katherine, Katelyn and other names among my students and colleagues.

Most Americans know very little about Latin American countries, their cultures and histories. This encouraged me to share more about my many cultures. It was no longer acceptable to me to be indifferent to identity falsehood. I am a blended Hispana who contains the world in her skin. I fit because I am many cultures. They all live in me. I appreciate when Americans understand me because it shows that they too can transcend cultural biases. I want them to see that I am made in the image of my ancestors and parents and that I am my own carving instead of the determination of the White dominant culture.

In making this choice to persist and claim my identity, I went in a different direction than my Aunt Bertha, the first of my extended family to immigrate here. She was one of the one million foreign-born Latinos living in the United States in 1960 (Flores 2017). When I visited her in California in 1974, she was working in the basement of a bank. She was proud of her role working with their computers. Although I never understood what she did, I knew she felt she had made it. But, as a teenager witnessing her, I saw a woman who hid in a perfect professional disguise until she retired. She never attended church because it was not in her nature, but she borrowed the look of the White American churchgoers. Her little purse always hung at her elbow; her classic pants fell flawlessly to brush her shining shoes. She wore glasses, permed her hair, and obsessed with flowery blouses with buttons in the front. She smiled at all White people, calling them "sweetie," something she did not do with others. Her fight was to be part of the cultural majority, to fit in the big community and avoid being treated as a less-than human being. She accepted quietly her experience of segregation and discriminatory rejection. I loved and admired my aunt for her strengths and strategic thinking, but not for internalizing racism. Yet, her times were different than mine. I would instead gather all that I had let go of about me, knowingly or unknowingly throughout my life, and embrace the more complex person I could be. With this energy change. I realized I needed to step up to contribute to the transformation of the cultural dialogue.

Becoming equals and communicating with mutual respect requires setting matters straight as well as doing a lot of forgiveness, having tremendous doses of compassion for human stupidity, leading one's own life, and learning from each other's cultures. When this type of human understanding happens, it shows in people's demeanor and their eyes like two shining stars. By the same token, I have to work on making sense of White discrimination because it contains a pattern of obliteration that originated with the European settlers, explorers, and colonists of the 16th century and earlier. Their beliefs legitimized the extermination and submission of other ethnic groups who were considered savage. The European settlers ignored other civilized cultures, the empires of Mesoamerica and the Andes. The English, Spanish, French and other dominant ethnic groups dehumanized more vulnerable populations under physiological and cultural pretexts that supported appropriation of the goods, land and power their victims possessed. This so-called civilized European mindset manifested a hidden and unacknowledged White savage who, driven by financial gains, produced a trail of blood on which White discrimination has continued to develop acts of domestic terrorism into the modern and contemporary eras.

Making sense of White discrimination is complex from my multiethnic position. Within me lives the history of European conquerors and colonizers, adventurers, builders of dreams, and the exterminators of nonwhite groups. My native genes, however, root me in the story of death and conquest and at the same time the making of the Incan Empire, an empire that subjugated other ethnic groups too. Both victims and conquerors are my ancestors. My skin shows the richness of my blood and history. I have the best seat in addressing discrimination because I am the result of many battles lived by colored and noncolored survivors. Memories of their actions, suffering, resistance, achievements, and transformation roll through to the present, where the battles continue.

As an educator engaged in dialogue of contemporary times with my students, I invite all to pause and ask themselves: What does it take to change a mindset nourished by malignant discrimination and lethality that resists human and civil rights for all? What does it take to build a mindset that honors and sustains human dignity through civility in this century? Perhaps we are simply too predetermined by Darwinian evolution—organic life that the mind cannot alter. Or can the mind alter the behaviors of discrimination engrained in the White savage? I ask this of myself too as a blended woman daring a journey of change.

The Meaning of "White Discrimination"

Hiring discrimination is "hardwired into the hiring system and that prejudice is clouding the screening of qualified applicants" (Gerdeman 2017). This is not news. Welcome to the party! This is the White savage acting upon whitening paths already walked by his ancestors. This is part of American heritage.

Whitening demands conformation to the culture imposed. Some White populations also suffer this discrimination when they do not represent the ideals of the dominant culture. What Putney and Putney (1964) labeled "a compulsory call" in rural America to conform to the majority or status quo still today deprives rural Americans and diverse ethnic groups. Since the time of the colonies, marginal groups have been deprived of their uniqueness and unable to develop their potential. Instead they conformed to a uniform entity by submitting their minds and souls. For Putney and Putney, this enforced an entrenched history in the social mindset:

> In that immense crowd which throngs the avenues to power in the United States, I found very few men who displayed that manly candor and masculine independence of opinion which frequently distinguished the Americans in former times.... When I survey this countless multitude of beings, shaped to each other's likeness.... The sight of such universal uniformity saddens and chills me, and I am tempted to regret that state of society which has ceased to be.... Every citizen, being assimilated to all the rest, is lost in the crowd (Putney & Putney 1964, 1).

Pressured to conform, White rural Americans have also become boxed in by a dangerous passivity that contrasts with the freedom of nonrural Americans and the creativity and resourcefulness that immigrants have in the current times. Their vulnerability allows President Donald Trump to maintain their support without a true engagement of minds. I know this America well because I taught and lived in Arkansas, where wealth still leans the traditional way. This population believes their despair, discontent, and disconnect is caused by the doings of immigrants such as myself. Yet their roots are found in the struggle to conform to the culture of the majority. Conforming limits the unique process of human evolution. However, this personal dissatisfaction is not the creation of immigrants, but a discontent founded in Americans' discrimination against other Americans.

As a woman who has been repeatedly discriminated against by White people in the United States, I have developed a certain equanimity on this old White act of domestic terrorism. But as a blended woman, "trigueña," I have realized I am free. I can exercise my freedom by joining, supporting and leading. I recognize that I am part of many worlds and eras and the meaning of discrimination is shaped by this wisdom. At work, this creates some confusion, newness, and knowledge about incarnating many cultures all equally valuable and integrated within me. I am like meaning, layered up by time. Meaning, as Tronick says:

> Is not one thing—one meaning. Meaning is a layered flow over time of the different meanings emerging from the multiple levels and processes that make meaning. Meaning is a laminated polysemic flow or bundle that affects itself as it flows into the future. Yet, this flow of meanings has to be

> assembled by individuals into a coherent sense of themselves in the world, into what I call a stay of consciousness (Tronick 2009, 87).

Thus, the meaning for me of White discrimination rests upon my recollected memories, healed wounds, resistance, advancements, and strong conviction that I am as good as any other human with the potential to grow. This awareness prompts me to evolve and to consolidate a stronger position from which I am able to serve my students and engage with colleagues.

My experiences of discrimination at work, in my immediate and at large environments, have made me alert to many forms of discrimination (direct, dismissive, mockery, judgments, etc.), but, by purposely owning the complexity of my life and doing something about it, I have become more content and better able to help the diverse population of students who live the tensions of discrimination. Discrimination, as an experience charged with emotions and values, affects the formation of the self. As Porges points out, these psychological processes mold our sense of self, shape our capacity to create relationships, and define our sense of safety (Porges 2009). Without safety, the self could enter a stage of disarray, leading to camouflaging, high alertness, depression, or paralysis (to name a few). Discrimination triggers fear that can prompt activation of defense mechanisms ranging from submission to radical violence.

My American Dream, and Those of Others

So how would one go about engaging the mind of a discriminator who has not yet incorporated the value of human equality? What would I say to this person? That God made us in his image, colorful and all equal? That there is a long blood-stained narrative of degrading other humans that is a projection of the oppressor's fears and interests? A mind that has not yet evolved to perceive the wider reality of human beings would respond with limited awareness and could turn to violence as his safety is disturbed.

Aunt Bertha adopted a quiet attitude of conformity that made her invisible. That provided safety for her and her family at a cost of self-denial and submission that is unbearable to me. I lead to support the younger generations of students and professionals who face the threats of today's whitening. Nowadays, safety increasingly fluctuates as political impasses heighten governmental and social divisiveness. I have seen some of my Hispanic students on alert—though DACA is not only about Hispanics—when Trump moved to terminate DACA (National Immigration Law Center). Their uncertainty grew together with their anxiety. Their sense of safety was unstable. With them in mind, I offered a course in Latin American culture and civilization entitled "Mujeres Peligrosas/Dangerous

Women." We read two novels by Elena Poniatowska, *Dos Veces Única* and *Leonora*. These novels and accompanying student research showed the great history of Mexico, the arts, battles for hegemony, discrimination, political changes, women's participation and corruption. Hispanic students with Mexican heritage learned that they came from an ancestral and wise culture; White students also learned. The course offered some mental safety to create, organize, communicate, support one another, and engage more in shaping their journeys. We developed cross-generational support as a ladder to reach their aims and beautiful dreams.

It takes a lot of giving to support the new generations of colorful humans, which also includes Black and White students. As my students reveal the impact of Trump's attacks against otherness, my vigilance increases. Otherness is where I live and where many of my Queens students live too. My vigilance made me reorganize my environment, shift myself, grow quickly, and improve my reality even as, or because, the current legitimization of whiteness grows. When he says that he speaks to his base, to which I do not conform, he undermines the national narrative that once enticed and included me and my students as well as other immigrants—the American Dream (Merriam–Webster.com Dictionary, Oxford Dictionary, Library of Congress). For our beautiful and costly dreams, we pay with labor, education, investments, stressed lives, and money that we bring from our countries to sustain our daily lives and actions. Nothing is given, but rather earned. Yet, we are discounted and considered the enemy.

The current president sees Hispanics as savage, yet he is unable to see that he embodies the White savage and its historical ideology. What safety can exist under this political whitening? Trump's discourse breaks with the narrative of the American Dream that past and new citizens have held dear throughout generations since the Declaration of Independence's vow "that all Men are created equal, that they are endowed by their Creator with certain unalienable Rights, that among these are Life, Liberty and the Pursuit of Happiness" (Library of Congress). Many "Dreamers" are, in fact, the result of their parents reaching to achieve the American Dream.

Part of the American Dream is the "social ideal that stresses egalitarianism [this implies safety for all] and especially material prosperity" (Merriam–Webster.com Dictionary). Yet Trump's whitening affects the core existence of citizens who held and hold this dream as a beacon for their future progress. Citizens like me, my students, and my colleagues at Queens University of Charlotte. Trump uses whitening as a political strategy to appeal to supporters and unify his allies. However, there is nothing to gain in self-denial or submission and the emptiness and darkness this causes. Instead, there is a lot to gain in activating dreams that stimulate personal and civic growth through education and social engagement; integration brings safety for all. To evolve together into the next level of civic consciousness is my American dream. I have learned to help make this dream. I will focus on being part of inclusive experiences that better the U.S. culture instead of accepting discrimination as the status quo at work or in any other area of life. How poor/limited that would be!

The White discrimination of 2019 might cause fear and incite those perceived as "other" to camouflage themselves. Still, I find hope in other strong responses, such as the unprecedented participation of women in the current 116th Congress: 102 women serving. I am hopeful that inclusive participation and purposeful integration might lead us to a higher level of consciousness. The freshness of alternative thinking, listening to ideas that compete and complement, can enable new knowledge and a higher sense of awareness that could see all colorful humans enhancing a healthier future with our shared wisdom. Valuing discourse that elevates the self and the mind, I expect to pursue and support the dreams of my students and colleagues for a beautiful life in this America that we create together. The first step to take is to quiet the absurdity of an administration that calls for whitening an America that is a melting pot. This diverse America needs to see itself in the mirror and learn to like itself. With that, we can start the process of transforming consciousness and integrating races and cultures. Our safety depends on our decisions, discourses, relations, and the world we imagine.

Sources

Flores, A. 2017. "Facts on U.S. Latinos, 2015, Statistical Portrait of Hispanics in the United States." *Pew Research Center*, September 18, 2017. pewhispanic.org/2017/09/18/facts-on-u-s-latinos.

Gerdeman, D. 2017. "Minorities Who 'Whiten' Job Résumés Get More Interviews." *Harvard Business School Working Knowledge*, May 17, 2017. hbswk.hbs.edu/item/minorities-who-whiten-job-resumes-get-more-interviews.

Library of Congress. (n.d.) "The American Dream." loc.gov/teachers/classroommaterials/lessons/american-dream/students/thedream.html.

Merriam–Webster.com Dictionary. (n.d.) "American Dream." Accessed on January 11, 2019, at merriam-webster.com/dictionary/American%20dream.

Merriam–Webster.com Dictionary. (n.d.) "Whiteness." Accessed on January 12, 2019, at merriam-webster.com/dictionary/whiteness.

National Immigration Law Center. 2018. "Status of Current DACA Litigation." Accessed January 7, 2019, at nilc.org/issues/daca/status-current-daca-litigation/.

Oxford Dictionary Online. (n.d.) "Whiteness." Accessed July 24, 2019, at lexico.com/definition/whiteness.

Oxford Dictionary Online. (n.d.) "American History." Accessed on January 13, 2019, at oxfordre.com/americanhistory/view/10.1093/acrefore/9780199329175.001.0001/acrefore-9780199329175-e-262.

Porges, S. 2009. "Reciprocal Influences Between Body and Brain in the Perception and Expression of Affect: A Polyvagal Perspective." In *The Healing Power of Emotion: Affective Neuroscience, Development, and Clinical Practice*, edited by Diana Fosha, Daniel J. Siegel and Marion F. Solomon, 27–54. New York: Norton.

Putney, S., & Putney, G.J. 1964. *The Adjusted American: Normal Neuroses in the Individual and Society.* New York: Harper & Row.

Tronick, E. 2009. "Multilevel Meaning Making and Dyadic Expansion of Consciousness Theory: The Emotional and the Polymorphic Polysemic Flow of Meaning" In *The Healing Power of Emotion: Affective Neuroscience, Development, and Clinical Practice* edited by Diana Fosha, Daniel J. Siegel, & Marion F. Solomon, 86–111. New York: Norton.

The Fight Against White Privilege

Mark E. Attucks Sr.

Imagine working all your life for what you consider the pinnacle of career success. For me, it was selection for a federal Senior Executive Service (SES) position. My emotions went from excitement to nervousness and then to pride when I learned of my selection for an SES position with the Department of Transportation Office of Inspector General (DOT/OIG) in 2014 after less than four years as a government employee.

The SES is made up of almost 8,000 political and career professionals above the GS-15 pay grade. The SES minimum salary is $127,914. For governmental hiring, there are two processes that potential employees can go through: (1) a background check for suitability, which is mandatory for all potential employees, and (2) a background check for security clearance, which applies only to those who have a need for a security clearance. With background checks for suitability, the employer is looking for past indicators that demonstrate reliability, trustworthiness, and ultimately suitability for positions of public trust, which are sensitive positions relating to protection of national security. The suitability-determination process provides for due process. If any issues surface, the employer must present them to the applicant and provide adequate time for the applicant to respond. Then a neutral party must review the facts, and either the applicant is determined unsuitable or hired. Allowing an applicant to see and respond to negative elements is important not only because of due process but also because the government is, frankly, known for making mistakes.

After experiencing one of the best days of my life with my selection for a coveted position, my world came crashing down. My selection was rescinded. Although I met all the prerequisites for the conditional job offer, the agency determined that I was unsuitable. Without any explanation of why the job offer was rescinded, I was left to figure out on my own what had happened to my dream job.

Knowing that a background check had been completed for my first government position, I submitted a Freedom of Information Act request for my records and discovered that the information in my record was incorrect. The investigator back then had transposed the last two digits of my Social

Security number. The record also referenced an arrest and dismissal that had occurred many years before. Though the investigator's mistakes had not affected getting my first or second government job, I suspected they were why the DOT/OIG job was rescinded.

Now, how could I prove this? How could a lower-graded employee, without a law degree, take on a huge federal agency? With the help of an attorney, I filed a U.S. Merit Systems Protection Board (MSPB) appeal because DOT/OIG had made an illegal suitability determination. Although DOT/OIG's internal documents showed that they had rescinded the job offer based on suitability, officials successfully argued before the MSPB that their action amounted to a non-selection, which falls outside of the purview of the board. Given that the DOT/OIG has never had a Black, male senior executive, I decided to file an Equal Employment Opportunity Commission (EEOC) complaint for discrimination. Unbelievably, the agency did an about-face. Officials now stated that their hiring decision was not discriminatory in nature because they selected me for the job knowing my race but then rejected me based upon suitability. Court documents from them stated that I was not hired because I "was not a good fit for their Agency." The agency's strategy was to talk out of both sides of its mouth: To the MSPB, it said the decision was not based on suitability factors but was a non-selection. However, in response to the EEOC complaint, the agency said it was not discriminatory but based upon suitability. It became painfully clear that agency officials knew that, if they had genuine concerns about anything within my background, they would have had to give me a chance to address the concerns. Mind you, I had completed 20 years of honorable military service and was working my second federal job.

The discriminatory actions by DOT/OIG against me illustrate the consequences of unconscious bias.[1] Unconscious bias is a form of prejudice in favor of or against a person or a group compared with another in a way that is unfair or illegal. This form of discrimination is typically subtle or covert, for example, disqualifying applicants with ethnic-sounding names or women candidates. This is why, 50 years since the passage of the Civil Rights Act of 1964, its protections are needed more than ever.

[1] In a 2016 article titled "Feds urged to fight 'unconscious bias' in hiring and promotions," Washington Post columnist Joe Davidson described efforts by Beth Cobert, then acting director of the U.S. Office of Personnel Management, to address unconscious bias in federal hiring, which she called "one of the most challenging barriers to diversity and inclusion."

Birth of the EEOC

During the Civil Rights Movement in the 1960s, African Americans demanded the protections of the Fourteenth Amendment of the U.S. Constitution. The Fourteenth Amendment, in part, guarantees "equal protection of the laws." On August 28, 1963, Martin Luther King Jr. delivered his "I Have a Dream" speech. He famously stated, "I have a dream that my four little children will one day live in a nation where they will not be judged by the color of their skin, but by the content of their character." The following year, President Lyndon Johnson signed the Civil Rights Act of 1964. This landmark law established certain protections within Title VII. That same year, Johnson also established the U.S. Equal Employment Opportunity Commission (EEOC), whose charge is enforcing federal laws that make it illegal to discriminate against a job applicant or an employee because of the person's race, color, religion, sex (including pregnancy, gender identity, and sexual orientation), national origin, age (forty or older), disability or genetic information. The law also stipulates that it is illegal to discriminate against someone because they complained about discrimination, filed a charge of discrimination, or participated in an employment-discrimination investigation or lawsuit.[2] The protections of the law and the authority of the EEOC apply to most employers with at least fifteen employees (twenty employees in age-discrimination cases). Most labor unions and employment agencies are also covered. The laws apply to all types of work situations, including hiring, firing, promotions, harassment, training, wages and benefits. According to the EEOC, in fiscal year 2018, there were 76,418 charges filed. The most concerning of the data shows that, in 2018, 32.2 percent of cases were for race discrimination.[3]

Service Above Self

Military service is ingrained within my DNA, dating all the way back to my ancestor Crispus Attucks, who was the first person to fight and die for America's freedom during the American Revolutionary War. Ever since then, an Attucks has served in the military. I followed the footsteps of my father, who is a Marine, into the Air Force. I served 20 years within the Air Force, focusing on security and finance, stateside and abroad.

---

[2] Learn more about the types of discrimination prohibited by federal law on the EEOC's website (eeoc.gov/laws/types/index.cfm).

[3] Fiscal year 2018 enforcement and litigation data are on the EEOC website (eeoc.gov/eeoc/newsroom/release/4-10-19.cfm).

During my time in the military, I had the privilege to serve with people from all walks of life. I will never forget being in basic training and meeting one of my fellow trainees from the sticks of South Dakota who had never had a conversation with a Black person before. Or, one of the trainees wanting to touch my hair to feel the consistency differences. In all my years of service, I do not recall experiencing any racial animus. I am honored to have brothers and sisters of all colors throughout the country. But this bubble was burst as I prepared to retire from the military and find employment as a civilian in the federal government.

The Air Force Personnel Center (AFPC) provides an assessment of your jobs, duties, responsibilities, level of leadership, span of control, and education to provide a comparative projective GS paygrade. When I received my assessment from AFPC in 2005, they had rated my extensive experience and education only at a GS-9 level, but I was operating at least at a GS-12 level.

There are two major challenges facing minority government employees, especially African Americans. The first is enlisted military bias. Although most enlisted military members have just as much, if not more, education and possess a tremendous amount of leadership experience, they have a very difficult time coming into the federal government within the senior paygrades of GS-9 through GS-15.[4] However, military officers, who are majority White, enter these senior grades as a common practice.[5] The second major challenge is depressed opportunities. According to the Office of Personnel Management, in 2010 the federal workforce was 18 percent Black, 66 percent White, 8 percent Hispanic, 6 percent Asian/Pacific Islander and 2 percent American Indian/Alaskan Native.[6] That same year, Black workers held 24 percent of the jobs in grades GS-1 through GS-9 but only 15 percent of positions in grades GS-9 through GS-15. By comparison, White workers held 59 percent of the positions in grades GS-1 through GS-9 and 72 percent of positions in grades GS-9 through GS-15. The data clearly show that Black workers are disproportionately hired at lower pay

---

[4] The OPM provides federal employment demographics every 10 years based on census data (opm.gov/policy-data-oversight/data-analysis-documentation/federal-employment-reports/demographics/2010/table2mw.pdf).

[5] Air Force data show that, out of 58,102 officers, 46,082 identify as White (diversity.defense.gov/LinkClick.aspx?fileticket=gxMVqhkaHh8%3D&portalid=51).

[6] OPM data shows that the federal workforce is overwhelmingly White. Black federal workers are disproportionately hired and kept in the lower paygrades, which equates to lower salaries and less authority (opm.gov/policy-data-oversight/data-analysis-documentation/federal-employment-reports/demographics/2010/table2mw.pdf).

grades, which results in less job advancement and income over the course of their careers.

Needless to say, the AFPC assessment, which failed to take into account my level of leadership, experience and education, made my decision to pursue private-sector employment easier.

Private Sector Discrimination

After retiring from the Air Force, I accepted a position as a distribution center executive for the mega-retailer Target. I was one of three Black executives on a team of 25. I was the only executive who had retired from the military. The primary prerequisite for this job was proven leadership skills. Given my 20-year career as a senior leader in the Air Force, my leadership skills and experience far surpassed those of any of the executives within the building, if not the entire distribution pyramid.

I soon discovered that the discussion of salary is taboo in the private sector. However, before learning this little piece of intel, I had a discussion with a peer executive. He was White, fresh out of college, and without a lick of leadership experience. Not only did he make $10,000 more than I did, but he also made more than the other two Black executives (one was a Naval Academy graduate and former naval officer.)

I determined that this position was not conducive to my long-term career plans, so I interviewed and was offered a transfer to Omaha, Nebraska. I was the first and only Black Target executive in the Midwest. The executive team of 750 was highly homogenous. I was excited about the prospects of making a positive impact, and the transfer came with a $20,000 pay increase. I was responsible for the entire state of Nebraska and western Iowa.

When I conducted my weekly store visits, while driving a new Cadillac Escalade ESV, I was either pulled over or followed *every time* by the state police. This harassment necessitated calling either my wife or my mother so that they were aware of what was going on in the event that something were to happen to me while out within the rural areas of Nebraska. I complained to my district leadership peers (all White) and my boss (also White), who was based out of Denver, Colorado. During my two-year assignment, I never received a ticket.

Incredibly, during one regional visit, my boss and two other district leaders were riding with me when, as usual, I was followed by the state police and pulled over. However, the officer was unaware that I had passengers with me. My colleagues were incredulous that this had been happening to me, despite my complaints for a year and a half that this harassment had become a part of my life.

This incident, as well as my superior performance, led to my selection by the CEO to oversee the pivotal entry of Target into offshore markets. I was tapped to provide leadership during the creation and staffing of its new stores in Hawaii. While I was waiting to begin this vital assignment, someone in the corporate office inadvertently sent an Excel file containing all executive salaries. It showed a significant pay disparity between executives of color and their White counterparts.

On the heels of this discovery began my salary negotiation for the Hawaii assignment. This process was very tense because the company wanted to pay me below what I deserved to be paid to live there. Armed with salary data, cost-of-living data, and knowledge, from an inside source, that I was their only option, I stayed fast on my salary demands, which the company eventually agreed to after four months. Within five months, under my leadership, we successfully opened three stores on two Hawaiian Islands. Two of them generated the most sales in one year of any of Target's 1,700 stores: $120 million and $90 million.

About a year and a half after the last store opened, I began hearing complaints from leadership that my "high" salary presented challenges to the contractual agreement of a mainland transfer after two years. Target wanted me to agree to stay another year. Knowing that my salary would always be an issue, I had very little confidence that a transfer would occur, even if I extended my stay in Hawaii, and I suspected that the more likely scenario would be the company cutting my position.

Federal Sector Discrimination

Another form of subtle or covert racism is White privilege, also known as "like me" bias. White privilege is an institutional set of benefits granted to those who resemble the people who dominate the powerful positions within our institutions. One of the primary privileges is by having greater access to power and resources than people of color do. Nowhere is this more evident than within the political juggernaut that is the federal government. The federal government, especially at the most senior levels, is overwhelmingly White and male.

White privilege and unconscious bias are so prevalent within the federal government that it necessitated in January 2010 the commissioning of a workgroup by the EEOC to identify the obstacles that hinder equal employment opportunities for African Americans. This workgroup identified seven obstacles. The first said: "Unconscious biases and perceptions about African Americans still play a significant role in employment decisions in the federal sector." The workgroup noted "that discrimination today tends to be more subtle and can often be directly attributable to unconscious bias."[7]

When I was seeking to relocate from Hawaii, I decided to pursue employment within the federal government. I was fortunate to be offered a position as a regional chief financial officer (CFO) for the Department of Veterans Affairs (a GS-13 position with promotional potential). Though the VA is the second-largest department within the federal government, I was the only Black CFO.

Federal hiring policy allows a selectee with superior qualifications to request to come into the government at the higher paygrade. My Target responsibilities, duties and salary were superior qualifications that should have resulted in approval of starting as a GS-14. However, my White, female supervisor decided that she would not recognize my superior qualifications, which resulted in a pay cut of over $50,000. Conversely, she hired my White, male peer as a GS-14 and established the expectation that I cover his functional errors whenever he was out of the office, but he was not expected to reciprocate. This discriminatory bias prompted me to file an EEO complaint. I won the case.

More of the Same

The equal pay law makes it illegal for an employer to pay different wage rates based on sex, race or ethnicity. In the winter of 2016, I was selected for a SES position with the Department of Justice. However, before I was able to start, President Donald Trump was elected and immediately implemented a hiring freeze. In May 2017, I was contacted by my new supervisor and informed that Attorney General Jeff Sessions had signed a hiring exemption due to the criticality of my position. I was offered a salary that I thought was low for the duties and responsibility that the job entailed. I shared my reservation with the human-resources specialist, who, in turn, told me that I needed to speak with my soon-to-be supervisor. I contacted the supervisor, and she told me that a 6 percent salary increase was department policy. I accepted the position and offer to come onboard as a deputy director. Although the Department of Justice has almost 200,000 employees, there are only two Black executives in the Justice Management Division. My office is led by a director, and I am one of two deputy

[7] The EEOC African American Workgroup Report (eeoc.gov/federal/reports/aawg .cfm) identified the following obstacles to equal opportunities: (1) unconscious bias, (2) inadequate mentoring and networking opportunities, (3) insufficient training and development assignments, (4) narrow recruitment methods, (5) discouragement, (6) education inequality, and (7) inadequate regulation and enforcement.

directors. My position description is the same as the other deputy director's position description.

In 2018, the director who hired me was removed from her position, and her boss became our reporting official. During this period, I received a performance evaluation that was less than what I had earned. I was told that an excellent evaluation was a good evaluation and that not everyone can receive an outstanding rating. She gave me an envelope that had my bonus and salary increase. She also gave me my peer deputy's unsealed envelope to leave on his desk. Curiosity got the best of me, and I discovered that he was making over $30,000 more than me, and his bonus was exponentially more than mine. The kicker is that, during a conversation with one of my direct reports, I discovered that even he makes more than I do. Having learned this, I had my administrative officer pull payroll data for all my direct reports, and, to my astonishment, every one of them makes more than me.

Now, before I tell you what happened next, there are two things you need to know. First, U.S. Department of Justice Order 1202, Executive Resources Management, dated November 26, 2013, provides a process for seeking pay parity above 10 percent for initial pay setting of career SES. Any percentage in excess of 10 percent requires approval by the attorney general or deputy attorney general. (Remember, Sessions signed my exception.) Second, presidential Executive Order 13714, dated December 15, 2015, mandates "for initial pay setting and pay adjustments, as appropriate, for career SES appointees to result in compensation exceeding the rates of pay, including locality pay, of their subordinate GS employees." This simply means that employees taking their first SES positions must, by law, make more money than those who work for them, which, at its core, makes complete sense.

I perceived what was happening as a clear violation of the law and a concern that anyone can relate to: your subordinates making more money than you are. Boy, was I so wrong. The leadership acted as if I shouldn't have brought this issue up because I had accepted their salary offer, to which I responded, "because I was told that my offer was consistent with every SES offer!"

"I wish you wouldn't have said anything and let the SERB fix it," the official said.

What a joke!

SERB stands for Senior Executive Review Board, the department body that is charged annually with reviewing salaries for pay equity and recommending performance awards and salary increases. My package, with salary, went before the SERB for the first time in December 2017 (seven months after receiving my illegal salary) and again in December 2018. Neither SERB review seemed to notice and certainly didn't correct the glaring pay discrepancy. But there I was being told, "I wish you wouldn't have said anything and let the SERB fix it."

After several months, I was finally told that my salary would be corrected "prospectively and not retroactively sometime in January." Allow me to give you a little context about why the "sometime in January" part is so important. My agency knew that I had been applying to law schools and was waiting on the schools' decision letters. I believed, and therefore they believed, that, if accepted into law school, I would be starting in January—meaning I would be leaving my job in December. So, their decision to correct my salary "prospectively and not retroactively sometime in January" meant that I would get absolutely nothing.

When the senior leader informed me of this decision, I had two questions: (1) "How would you feel if this had happened to you?" and (2) "How would you have handled this if it had happened to you?" (I had heard that they were upset by how I handled this.) I didn't even receive an answer to my first question.

"This is not about how I would feel," he replied.

I also asked if he thought that it was appropriate for me to make less than my direct reports. He said that nothing was done improperly, that the Obama executive order was a guide, that they have time to bring salaries up to the appropriate level mandated by the executive order, and that I was making less than my subordinates for only one year (as if that is not bad enough).

I again reminded him that, as the documentation that I had given them clearly shows, I have always made less and currently still make less than my subordinates. When I returned to my office, I sent him an e-mail memorializing our conversation and asked him to correct anything for the record that was not accurate. He responded stating that he was in error when he stated that I made less than my subordinates for only a year, that he did not say that the executive order was a guide, that my pay was correctly set, and that sometime in January my pay would be adjusted to above my subordinates.

Obviously, I am not satisfied with this response or actions, so this is yet another potential legal issue that I will need to pursue.

Putting My Money Where My Mouth Is

After working with attorneys on my own legal issues and working at EEOC, which is an attorney-centric agency, I developed a disdain for attorneys—not the profession itself, per se, but the people who represented the profession. It did not matter whether they were private-sector attorneys, whom I saw as money hungry, or government attorneys, whom I observed to be incompetent, for the most part.

However, while working at the EEOC, two things occurred that changed the trajectory of my life. First of all, I was sickened by the enormous number of discrimination cases. Some cases—you would have thought we, as a society, were stuck in a time warp and still in the 1950s and 1960s. Second was the hands-on legal experience that I got, teaching myself, while I dealt with my litigation against DOT/OIG. I gained so much experience and confidence that I eventually was able to go *pro se* in addition to helping others.[8] An inside calling started whispering about me becoming an attorney to be able to assist people, in particular with litigation against the federal government.

I took a leap of faith in the spring of 2016 by going back to school to earn a legal studies undergraduate degree to ensure that I truly had the aptitude within the legal field. At the age of 52, I completed my degree with a 3.9 GPA, and that solidified my passion of becoming an attorney.

However, I was a bit naïve, because I was not completely knowledgeable about this little test called the Law School Aptitude Test (LSAT). That little test proved to not be my friend; although I scored my personal best, it was still less than ideal. There are ample data available showing that standardized tests are biased against people of color, and this is true for the LSAT especially.[9] In addition, Black students find getting accepted into law school a very daunting task. In fact, 49 percent of Black law school applicants do not receive even one acceptance.[10] I found out how daunting a task getting into law school can be. With 35 years of varied work experience, an excellent undergraduate GPA and a commitment to quit my six-figure job, I applied to 22 law schools all over the country. After getting several denials, I e-mailed an admissions officer and asked for some feedback. He instructed me to call him, which I did. He said that, although I had great credentials and work experience, my age was a negative indicator because of the risk of not successfully completing the program and future employability based on my salary expectations. At that juncture, I changed my strategy and

[8] Litigants or parties representing themselves in court without the assistance of an attorney are known as *pro se* litigants.

[9] Christopher Jencks and Meredith Phillips dive into test score disparities in their book *The Black–White Test Score Gap*.

[10] The 2019 article "Do Law Schools Limit Black Enrollment With LSAT?" describes the uphill battle many Black people face with getting into law school (insidehighered.com/admissions/article/2019/04/15/study-argues-law-schools-limit-black-enrollment-through-lsat).

researched law schools that offer conditional-acceptance programs. I was one of eight applicants who got invited to participate in the Western Michigan University Cooley School of Law program. All eight invitees were people of color. Out of the eight, only two of us were extended an unconditional offer into law school. So, what a long and stressful process, but it is a continuance of the dream!

The Obama Effect

There are some who argue that we are in a post-civil rights era and that the protections afforded by the Civil Rights Act are no longer needed. They use as an example the presidency of Barack Obama. This is a fallacy; the protections of the Civil Rights Act are needed more than ever because the data show that the number of race-based discrimination cases filed with the EEOC increased during Obama's terms in office. Indeed, within the federal government, the "good old boy" network is as pervasive as it ever has been, especially since the Obama administration. The mindset for some of the covert-racist sort is to take back any perceived losses that occurred during that administration. In addition, the election of President Donald Trump and his rhetoric have emboldened those with racist agendas to become more boisterous. The "Make America Great Again" (MAGA) mantra that Trump initiated assumes that America somehow lost its greatness and seeks to return to a time before the disenfranchised had the protections of the Civil Rights Act. Furthermore, those who support the principles of MAGA, who are largely White, male and without a college degree, believe incorrectly that people of color are responsible for their current plight. In reality, what makes us different as a nation makes us a positive example of diversity for the world. Therefore, it is unfortunate that the election of a Black president didn't wipe the slate clean and, in fact, heightened resentments.

More Work Is Still Needed

In conclusion, in the 53 years since the signing of the Civil Rights Act of 1964, much progress has been made; however, the protections to level the playing field with employment and promotional opportunities for all individuals, to provide enforcement of the laws for everyone, and to combat unconscious bias and perceptions against certain classes of people remain relevant as ever. EEOC data clearly show that the number of discrimination cases is increasing, not decreasing. Discrimination cases constitute the largest category of all court cases. The lack of African Americans in senior-level positions within the government points to a void of equal opportunities for all. However, entities taking a stand, such as the EEOC African American Workgroup, and the Office of Personnel Management actually addressing the concept of unconscious bias in a 2016 memorandum to all federal agencies provides hope that we, as a nation, can overcome our dark past of discrimination. In the words of Dr. Martin Luther King Jr., "Darkness cannot drive out darkness; only light can do that. Hate cannot drive out hate; only love can do that." In a society where everyone is treated equally and provided the same opportunities, the protections of the Civil Rights Act of 1964 would no longer be needed.

In Academia, the Gates of Entry and Advancement Are Guarded by Those Who Uphold White Supremacy

Michael A. Moreno

Pulitzer-winning author Junot Díaz issued an indictment of creative writing MFA programs in the *New Yorker* in 2014.[1] Díaz described applying to programs he knew nothing about, matriculating into one and quickly discovering the "unbearable too-whiteness." People of color who have suffered through or abandoned MFA programs knew what he was talking about all too well. A handful of them wrote blogs and tweets about their experiences in the blinding whiteness of MFA workshops. They wrote about their classmates objecting to their use of their native or family tongues. They wrote about professors who were unwilling or incapable of leading productive discussions about writing about race. They wrote about how isolated they felt in their so-called communities of writers. National Public Radio later ran a segment that expanded on Díaz's contention that writers of color need to come together and establish new writing groups and organizations that support minorities the way MFA programs support White writers.

I don't think such groups or programs are a bad idea in and of themselves. I've benefited from more than one. In fact, I met my co-editors on this book by submitting my writing to their journal, *Label Me Latina/o*, which is explicit in its aim to publish Latinx writers. Affinity groups do good work. But they certainly are not the solution to a systemic problem.

---

[1] In 2018, during the #MeToo movement, multiple women accused Díaz publicly of behaving in ways that were sexually and verbally abusive. The Massachusetts Institute of Technology, where he teaches creative writing, investigated and cleared him to continue teaching. The Boston Review, for which he served as an editor, also allowed him to retain his position, but other editors resigned in protest. Though he volunteered to resign as chair of the Pulitzer Prize board, the organization, after its own investigation, determined he should not be removed.

University administrators and faculty members who refuse to stomp out racist rhetoric—by students, colleagues and others—must be held accountable for upholding White supremacy and creating a hostile or even unsafe environment for people of color. Teachers of writing, especially, should be able and willing to identify and dismantle racist arguments. If they can't or won't, they shouldn't have jobs teaching writing. Entertaining racist ideas even briefly lends them credibility; it also harms people of color who are present and, in many cases, forced to defend their humanity.

I say all this as a Latinx writer who attended the MFA program at and later taught in the college writing program at American University in Washington, D.C. I say this as a professor who has been harassed by racist students, undermined by racist colleagues and admonished by administrators who were offended and intimidated by my adherence to and performance of anti-racist pedagogy. I say this as someone who wants to make the halls of academia better—for students and for faculty.

My MFA experience was horrible, and I make sure to tell people about it all the time. I probably sound like a broken record. But I'm not going around telling my story for my own benefit. It's not like American University is going to issue me a refund, though it should. I tell my story because academics, even those who claim to be progressive, both consciously and unconsciously maintain White supremacy. I tell my story because the radical change the academy needs won't be born from silence.

Getting There

I was not your typical young, upper-middle-class MFA'er. I grew up as a migrant farmworker in the South. I basically raised myself, and at times my younger siblings, while laboring in cotton fields and gins. As an adult, I worked in information technology and did some agricultural consulting in Africa. I attended college off and on when I had the money. When I was in my 30s, a grant and loans enabled me to return to school full time to finish my English undergraduate degree and begin to contemplate a life unlike any I'd ever known.

The University of Houston's English department was celebrated on campus because its graduate creative writing program had been for many years ranked as one of the best in the nation. The program's professors teach introductory courses, too, of course, and I felt fortunate to have access to them as an undergrad, even if, as rumor had it, the graduate program preferred to select students from other schools. I took undergraduate poetry with Tony Hoagland. This was the mid-2000s, and Hoagland was piling up recognition and prizes for his work, among them the Mark Twain Award from The Poetry Foundation. Though some of Hoagland's poems were regarded by many as amusing, he took class seriously. I sensed from the beginning, however, that he wasn't there at the head of the classroom for students like me. He was there for the White kids, like the young man who wrote a poem about a shit sandwich. Still, I appreciated the feedback I got from Hoagland on my poems. To this day, I credit him for emphasizing that Americans "like stuff" (meaning specifics) in their poetry.

When I decided I wanted to give graduate school a go, I emailed Hoagland, against my better judgment, to ask if he'd be willing to write a letter of recommendation. I would have been disappointed by—but certainly expected—a "no" from him, but he didn't even have the decency to say "no." Instead, I received what appeared to be an out-of-office message, though it wasn't labeled as such. It was one line and said something to the effect of him being away until 1969. I'm sure he thought it was funny.

Going for an MFA—becoming a writer—was a real leap, but I took it anyway. I applied to schools in California and Washington, D.C., where my wife thought she'd be able to find rewarding work. I was accepted by several programs that interested me, but, after living for so long on the margins, frequently and wrongly assumed to be undocumented despite my Lubbock, Texas, birth certificate, I was enamored with the idea of attending American University in D.C. The name was everything. It was the cred I needed to be viewed as an American—and an American writer—or so I naïvely thought.

Coming to American

The first formal American University MFA event I attended was at a lovely home just outside of D.C. near the start of the fall semester. The libations flowed freely. There was a cake-decorating contest. I listened to 20-something second- and third-year White female students giddily gush about how supportive their thesis adviser was of their work. (This White male poet later would become my own thesis adviser. Indeed, he has mastered flattery.) I watched with curiosity as a White woman, who later taught my nonfiction classes, carried on comically about the best wines on the backyard cart. I did my best attempt at small talk, which I admit I am terrible at, while thinking, as Díaz put it in his *New Yorker* essay, "get me the fuck out of here." I could not imagine how I might one day become like these people, whose biggest concerns appeared to be getting pats on the back or chuckles for witticisms about booze. That event was the high point of my MFA experience. It was all downhill from there.

That November, Hoagland was honored at the Library of Congress. I went to his reading, during which he recited a poem that carried on about the deficiencies of rap music. Afterward, I went up to talk to him. He recognized me and was congenial. I congratulated him and told him that I was pursuing my MFA.

"We should be celebrating you," he said.

I later learned that I wasn't the only one side-eyeing Hoagland back then. At the 2011 Association of Writing Programs conference, Claudia Rankine gave a talk in which she described a conversation she had with him about one of his poems. In her talk, Rankine didn't call the poem racist, but she said that some readers perceived it to be racist. (Writer Syreeta McFadden, for National Public Radio, described it as bearing "the trappings of racist tropes, language encapsulating a very particularly biased imagination.") Rankine's colleague-to-colleague discussion with Hoagland didn't go very well, and he told her the poem was "for white people." Rankin wrote: "Did he mean it was for white people to see themselves and their thinking? He did not say that. He said it was for white people." Hoagland wrote a public response to Rankine's talk, telling the Jamaica-born writer that she is naïve about race.

Racism in the Classroom

The writing workshops at American University were eye-opening, but for all the wrong reasons. I learned from one White classmate that Latinos don't read. Multiple White classmates tried to equate their experiences as first-generation college graduates or with childhood poverty with the experiences of Black and Brown people.

My nonfiction professor made fun of aging British men who, as she put it, get "yellow fever" (marry Asian women). She also divulged that a Black student in our cohort was so incompetent that he was going to write only book reports for her. At several points, she noted, or perhaps threatened is more accurate, that her then-husband was some sort of security expert. So, yes, all the racist bullshit Díaz noted.

For one nonfiction course, taught by the professor mentioned above, I was working on a story about the murder of an undocumented farmworker on Maryland's Eastern Shore. When the professor told us to write a profile of someone, I decided to interview an immigration expert on campus. This source is a writer's delight. She is one of those Northeastern liberals who grew up riding horses, got arrested during demonstrations in Latin America, and was quick to criticize the Clinton administration's crack cocaine policies, not that I'd asked about that. During our interview, she talked at length about Americans' misconceptions about immigrants. She went on about how Jewish immigrants gained whiteness over time. She noted that certain subgroups of Jews—insular, ultra-Orthodox ones—are rarely viewed as a drain on the system the way Latin American immigrants are, but, in fact, often do rely on public assistance to support their large families. I quoted her saying something to that effect in my piece for my class, and my professor took umbrage. I repeatedly pointed out that she was objecting to a quote—my source's words, not my own. But she picked apart the piece and encouraged my classmates to do the same. When we took a short break, I went out to get a sip of water at the fountain, and she followed me.

"I'm sorry if we were hard on you in there," she said, "but, just so you know, I'm Jewish."

So was my source.

Thereafter, it seems, she made it her mission to make me as uncomfortable as possible during our workshop. I won't bore you with the litany of microaggressions. I'll just say that it was, without a doubt, a hostile learning environment.

When I was required to take a second class with this professor, the situation escalated. On several occasions, students made wholly insensitive comments about Latinos, and the professor did nothing. Paradoxically, she also encouraged us to ferret out stories about the marginalized. You know, to exploit them for their stories. Like, for example, the Asian woman she saw set herself on fire abroad. That was a story she liked to tell. Real cocktail party fodder.

Then things went from worse to worst. I submitted an assignment, due via email at 10 p.m. Friday for the next week's workshop, about two hours late. (I admit, I was perfecting it.) The professor wrote back: "Your paper is late. Please see the syllabus for the course policy on late papers." I pulled up the syllabus, which stated that late submissions would result in an "F" in the course. Mind you, she had never penalized White students who showed up to our workshop—our actual workshop!—without submissions for us to read. I knew whatever was going on had nothing to do with teaching new writers to be disciplined. Something more sinister was at play.

I sought the counsel of my thesis adviser, who at the time was also the MFA program chair. I was a grad student adjunct by then, so I also told my supervisor. No grad student can recover from an "F"—dropping out seemed to be my only option at that point. I didn't know what this would mean for my students. The program chair insisted I could complete the course and didn't have to drop out of school. I stayed. The professor deducted half a letter grade on my story. I got an A-minus on it.

I later learned that neither my thesis adviser nor my teaching practicum supervisor (both white, male and Jewish) had formally documented the incident. No university authorities ever contacted me. It was swept under the rug. I think this happened to a Black male classmate, too, but I was so worried about myself at the time that I didn't follow up with him. To this day, I regret that.

Against all reasonable expectations, it didn't stop there. The professor at some point tried to join my thesis committee. I was terrified, of course, but managed to avoid that nightmare. Another White Jewish woman on a temporary appointment did join my committee, and she was great. Still, even after graduating and becoming a regular adjunct, I faced the professor's insults. Once she told me I might be "more comfortable" teaching somewhere with a different kind of students. I'm guessing she meant Brown ones. At some point, I heard that she'd been granted tenure and had tweeted or emailed something to the effect of "Suck it, bitches."

Mind you, this is just one professor. There were others. During conversations with other writers of color from my cohort, I was reassured that my experience was not unique. Alliances were made, White students fed on the animus of their professors, and students of color either vanished or made it through worse for wear.

I Kept My Head Down—Until I Couldn't Anymore

During my first few years of teaching in the college writing program at American University, I stuck to material that was palatable for all. We read the university's common texts and handbooks. We talked about fallacies, using evidence to support your claims, and how to identify and counter faulty rhetoric. Things went pretty smoothly. My students wrote well-argued essays of little to no consequence.

Then White students on campus used the social media app Yik Yak to anonymously tell Black students to "go back to Africa." Then Donald Trump came down that escalator and launched his racist presidential campaign by calling Mexicans rapists. Then more Black men were shot by police. Then White students threw bananas and hung nooses to intimidate Black women on campus. Colin Kaepernick knelt. Protests erupted on campus. The university and the nation were becoming more dangerous for my students of color and for me.

I could no longer ignore the responsibility that comes with being at the front of the classroom. I could no longer justify spending time showing videos of bird mating dances or entertaining discussions about the students' trips to the National Zoo. I was obligated, by virtue of my position of influence, to do whatever I could to make my students aware of barriers for people of color, women and other marginalized groups. If I just filled my classes with innocuous readings, graded trivial arguments, and ignored injustice, I would be complicit. I would be perpetuating systems that regard me and many of my students as less than—and teaching my students to do the same. Playing it safe is dangerous.

I immersed myself in the literature of anti-racist pedagogy. I read up on best practices and first-person accounts. I assessed and confronted my own biases, of which there were many. I gathered stacks of studies and argumentative essays for in-class discussions on housing discrimination and the wealth gap, police shootings of Black men, student debt load, and various other timely topics relating to inequity and injustice. I committed to not just stomping out racist rhetoric but demonstrating to my students how they could do it too.

I anticipated that quite a few of my students wouldn't be eager to give much thought to their privileges, bigotry and prejudices, and I hoped that being transparent about the course themes from the beginning would give them fair warning. In fact, in an introductory email, before students even stepped foot in the classroom, I made clear what was in store. For my WRTG 101 seminar, titled "A More Just World," I wrote to students in a welcome email:

> I can tell you, based upon my experience, that students who enter this course with a genuine interest in equality, justice and anti-racism activism enjoy it very much. Those who are uncomfortable discussing systemic racism and their own prejudices and privileges enjoy it less. To paraphrase AU's vice president for campus life, Fanta Aw, your professors are responsible for ensuring safe classrooms—but not necessarily comfortable ones. If you are not interested in the topics listed above or unwilling to enter in good faith into this semester-long discussion about what it will take to create "a more just world," then I recommend that you drop this course and enroll in one with a theme that better suits you.

My hope, clearly, was that students who wanted to engage with these issues would stick around and that students who wanted to avoid them would pick another section. The department offered plenty of tame options, such as food, sports and fairy tales, all of which could have been taught using an anti-racist framework but, as far as I knew, at the time did not. I always had plenty of takers and usually a waiting list.

Courage Comes at a Cost

I knew I'd be asking students to make themselves vulnerable in classes that tackle injustice, so I made myself vulnerable by example. In her book *Teaching to Transgress: Education as the Practice of Freedom*, bell hooks wrote: "It is often productive for professors to take the first risk, linking confessional narratives to academic discussions so as to show how experience can illuminate and enhance our understanding of academic material" (21). On the first day of each class, for example, I told them I was an AU alumnus and had been trained in teaching writing as a graduate student there. I told them how, when I was in training, my White female professor told me that men of color should shave their facial hair and speak softly in the classroom so that White students would not feel intimidated. Standing there in front of them in a full beard, I explained that I had rejected that (seemingly well-meaning) advice, knowing full well that it would have consequences.

But making myself vulnerable came at a cost. After Donald Trump was elected, I started carrying my birth certificate. I was volunteering in my free time with DACA students at a community center in D.C. I knew the kids would be the targets of immigration-enforcement activities and that I could get entangled. Having grown up in a migrant family, I had lived through raids before. During one of my classes at AU, I mentioned carrying my birth certificate for the reason I just stated, and a student was so upset that they complained to my department head. I ended up having to go explain the situation: I am carrying it for my safety.

I have other examples of absurd student complaints, but I'll share just one more. One semester I had a male student who had been alternatingly absent and disruptive. I'd talked to him outside of class about his behavior. One day, when he did show up for class, he was up to his usual antics. Concerned that he was derailing the in-class discussion, I raised my voice with him. This apparently upset a White female student. She complained to my supervisor, who called me to his office and told me I should apologize to the complainant. This is the same supervisor who had previously told me it was OK to lean in when a student is being difficult. I'd explicitly asked him during my training after seeing my mentor do it and feeling uncertain about it. I pointed out the double standard. He still made me apologize to her, which I found to be both unnecessary and undermining of my authority.

Learning to Better Understand Themselves

There's an abundance of research about college students' experiences and biases, and I exposed my students to many of those studies. We read and discussed, for example, research by Nolan León Cabrera at the University of Arizona. One of his studies, from 2012, is about White male students minimizing racism and claiming that they experience reverse-racism. Cabrera wrote: "This sense of victimization corresponded to the participants blaming racial minorities for racial antagonism (both on campus and society as a whole), which cyclically served to rationalize the persistence of segregated, white campus subenvironments" (30). This provoked lively discussions about, for starters, students' experiences in fraternities and sororities. We also read and discussed Cabrera's 2012 study about allyship, for which he interviewed White male college students about their racial cognizance. One of the participants, Cabrera recalled, shared that he was meaningfully affected by a course that contended with the issues my courses covered. Cabrera wrote:

> While courses focusing on issues of race and racism were generally few and far between, such courses frequently had profound effects on those working through whiteness. For example, Josh's initial college classes avoided most issues of race; and because of his self-described white, conservative, suburban background, he held a number of views that he now considers racist (e.g., that racial inequality is a function of Black laziness). His awareness changed dramatically during his undergraduate experiences. He vividly remembered a class in which the professor not only taught about racial inequality, but also humanized Black people in the process (386).

To dispel the notion that only White men hold racial biases, we also read, among others, a study about Asian international students' perceptions of American minority populations by Zachary S. Ritter at the University of Redlands. Ritter interviewed Chinese, Japanese, and South Korean international students and found that most of them arrived in the U.S. with negative perceptions of African Americans and, in fact, learned in the U.S. to have negative perceptions of Latinos. There were many international students from Asia in my courses, and they were keenly interested in that paper—and some were brutally honest about their prejudices.

My students also dug into the literature on how their White teachers uphold White supremacy. They read, for example, a 2009 study by Bree Picower at New York University, who interviewed pre-service teachers about how their life experiences influenced their understanding of race and difference. Picower's description of one interviewee captures succinctly how many White people—and, in fact, many White students in my courses—employ their European ancestors' immigration stories to blame people of color for the inequity they experience. Picower wrote of that teacher-in-training: "Dawn described her father's experience of the American dream: he came here with nothing, worked hard, and made it. The implication is clear—if he could make it, anyone can. She used her family's Italian immigration story as the normative experience upon which all people should model success. Such a view upholds the dominant ideology of people of color as lazy and victims of their circumstances and helps teachers such as Dawn to perpetuate the myth of American meritocracy" (201). Among the ideological tools of whiteness employed by the White pre-service participants of Picower's study to maintain their hegemonic stories were (206–209):

- claiming that things are equal or at least better now, so additional anti-racism work is unneeded,
- claiming that racism is personal, not institutional, so systemic changes are unwarranted, and
- claiming that they treat people nicely, even citing the Golden Rule (to do unto others as you would have them do unto you), ultimately perpetuating their White innocence.

My students also looked at the literature on how prejudiced people manage to convince themselves that they are not all that prejudiced. They read, for example, a 2010 study by researchers at Tulane University and the University of Kansas, who exposed participants to social representations of prejudice to see how those representations influence their evaluations of their own prejudices. Ultimately, the researchers found that the participants were more likely to evaluate themselves as less prejudiced than their peers when they were exposed to representations of prejudice. The researchers wrote, "[T]he present research suggests that, at least on some occasions, people deliberately seek out exposure to these representations of prejudice in order to reduce threats to their unprejudiced self-images. This self-protective strategy may serve to make white Americans comfortable, but it may also create the space for them to convince themselves that their failings are minor, and that as long as they do not join the Ku Klux Klan or start burning crosses on people's lawns, they're doing just fine" (O'Brien et al. 2010, 940). I saw this a lot in the classroom. Students asserted, for example, their parents are undoubtedly racist, but they're not. Examining this study, and others like it, made them question such comforting comparisons.

In addition, these new writers learned, among other things, that students of color are disciplined more harshly than their White classmates, that racial discrimination and stigma have cellular and molecular effects that result in significant health disparities and premature death, that colorism and Western beauty standards result in exclusion and self-harm both in the U.S. and abroad, that no class is neutral, and that imposter syndrome and stereotype threat affect individuals' performance on examinations.

Ultimately, my hope was that, by exposing college students to scholarship about college students they would be more willing to put their own experiences and biases under the microscope—and write about them. With each passing day, they got better at evaluating peer-reviewed research, critiquing the researchers' methodologies, data analysis, and conclusions. They got better at finding flaws in rhetoric that justifies injustice. They learned that when the evidence doesn't support their position, they need to change their position. They learned how to be allies for the vulnerable and the marginalized. Ultimately, they wrote well-argued essays of consequence. (I urge you to read an essay by one of them, Jacqueline Lantsman, found in this book.)

Unsurprisingly, readings packed with quantitative and qualitative data and in-class discussions sometimes provoked students to lash out. Once a racist White male student was upset by something he read in our text, *Seeing White: An Introduction to White Privilege and Race* (Halley et al. 2011). He took a threatening posture and screamed in my face in the hallway in front of other faculty members, who, by the way, lacked the moral courage to intervene or even follow up with me. Once a racist White female student had her relatives and friends send me harassing emails. This is a tactic encouraged by the conservative group Turning Point USA, with which this student was affiliated. TPUSA maintains a watchlist of professors they say discriminate against conservative students. It has been criticized by the Anti-Defamation League and the Southern Poverty Law Center for playing footsy with White supremacists (ADL 2020; Kelley 2018). The student, once she returned from the Conservative Political Action Conference (more commonly known as CPAC), ultimately was removed from my class, but only after I dug up social media posts wherein she explicitly stated that she planned to disrupt the class to teach her liberal classmates a lesson. Others like her also clung to their racism to the very end. Once a racist White male student gave a last-day-of-class presentation arguing, in short, "immigrants are replacing us." He was echoing the flawed and dangerous rhetoric employed by those advocating for Brexit and the chants of neo-Nazis in Charlottesville, Va., both of which we'd discussed in class.

Absence of Leadership—and Acknowledgement

Unfortunately, I also have had more discouraging encounters with colleagues than I can count. I'll describe just a few for illustrative purposes. Once a racist White male colleague told me immigrants "are using up all the resources" in this country (Moreno 2018). Once a racist White female colleague told me she wished Central American migrants would fix their own countries so they wouldn't have to come here. She said it in anger when we were alone after I'd said publicly, during a faculty meeting, that we should teach students how to stomp out hateful rhetoric. She did not acknowledge the role of whiteness or U.S. policies in the Americas (Moreno 2018). Lastly, after being stopped by university police for no reason multiple times, I decided to start wearing a jacket and tie every time I went to campus. This became, apparently, a joke among my colleagues, despite my explanation for why I was doing it.

Over the years, I've sought out colleagues and administrators willing to partner with me to confront biases and White privilege in our department. I've written letters, given presentations, and met with people face to face. Nobody on campus has been willing to act in a meaningful way.

I understand that anti-racism work carries professional risks. Naturally, my AU colleagues who consider themselves allies also want to be accepted by peers, to be invited to their parties, to have their work promoted and so forth. But it does disappoint me that they are not willing to use their influence to make the radical reforms that will change the lives of countless current and future students and faculty members and that will make AU the kind of school they claim they want it to be.

Furthermore, I have accepted that my presence in the halls of the academy force my colleagues to reckon with how they got there and who they, deep down, are rooting for to come after them. I came from the fields. They came from Connecticut. OK, not all of them. Some are from Pennsylvania. (I jest.) I grew up around laborers, mechanics and truck drivers. They grew up around intellectuals, artists and bankers. I wasn't supposed to end up in the academy. They were. The 2002 poem that provoked a public debate between Hoagland and Rankine was titled "The Change." Hoagland's narrator describes watching a tennis match: "I couldn't help wanting the white girl to come out on top, because she was one of my kind, my tribe, with her pale eyes and thin lips and because the black girl was so big and so black, so unintimidated, hitting the ball like she was driving the Emancipation Proclamation down Abraham Lincoln's throat, like she wasn't asking anyone's permission." That is a confession about like-me bias that you won't hear on faculty hiring committees or tenure-and-promotion panels. But faculty demographics, salary data and other measurable outcomes speak volumes. When Hoagland was dying in 2018, he penned an essay in the magazine *The Sun* titled "The Cure for Racism is Cancer." In it, he wrote, "If you are white and doing well in America, a voice whispers to you incessantly, repeating that you deserve to be on top, that to profit is your just reward." When confronted by teachers like me, my colleagues no longer can tell themselves that they've fully earned their places. Some of us worked a lot harder for fewer rewards.

Faculty members from marginalized groups consistently report that they lack the support they need to be successful in their careers. Contingent faculty of color—that is, adjuncts like me—have additional complications: extraordinarily low pay (on average about $3,000 per class), semester-to-semester job insecurity, no health insurance, frequently irregular hours, distant job assignment locations, and lack of appropriate office space in which to meet with students. On top of that, as universities increasingly rely on part-time faculty, who are generally younger and more diverse than full-time faculty, to teach their core curricula and inflate their faculty diversity numbers, adjuncts end up doing a lot of what I call the social work of teaching. That is to say that we are the people to whom the undocumented, the harassed, the excluded and the hopeless confide. The uncompensated emotional labor, in all honesty, is crushing.

As painful as it was for me to know that my colleagues at AU were racist at worse or cowards at best, I hated most how they failed our students. Here's one heartbreaking example. During the final week of a semester, a Black female student (let's call her Lisa) sought my counsel after a classmate (let's call him John) had used the N-word during history class. (Lisa and John were in my writing class together that same semester.) John had been difficult in my class, so I was not surprised by the news. He was not a good student and didn't operate in good faith. (For example, one assignment required going to a Smithsonian museum. He toured the Trump White House with credentials secured by a relative.) Lisa was upset because their White female history professor failed to step forward and speak up when John used the N-word. Instead, the professor left it to the Black students and their allies to tell John that he was out of line. John faced no apparent consequences, and Lisa rightfully felt betrayed by the professor and the school. I won't get into how I came to learn about the N-word incident from John himself, but let's just say that it was surreal, and I still can't believe it happened. Ultimately, he admitted what he'd done. I went to my supervisor to see what we could do about the situation. She told me Lisa could file a bias report but that was it. Lisa transferred to a new school the next fall.

Leaving American

During the spring of 2018, I met twice with my new supervisor, a White woman who often uses Twitter to feign allyship, to discuss racist students' complaints. When we met the first time, she started tearing up when I was firm about my position. I backed off because I didn't want her to cry. (I also didn't want her White fragility to get me killed by campus cops, who, as I mentioned above, had stopped me for no reason before.) The second time we met, after she sat in on one of my classes, she provided her evaluation of my teaching with her office door open, which indicated to me that she felt unsafe being alone with me and that she was unconcerned about employee privacy. After some time passed, she tried to get me to come see her again, but I couldn't bear it. I didn't trust her to have an honest discussion about stomping out racism in the classroom. I didn't trust her to not get me killed by the police. I resigned. It was whiteness at work.

It is well documented that college students are more likely to lodge complaints against and give lower teaching evaluations of their faculty members of color than their White faculty members. Michael Messner at the University of Southern California in 2000 suggested "that it is not simply that women, and women and men of color, are being 'graded down' because of gender and/or racial bias students hold; it is also that white males are actually being 'graded up.'" Indeed, a movement is under way to advocate for different methods for evaluating faculty effectiveness. "Holding instructors to high standards is important, and student feedback is relevant," explains Northwestern University law professor Michelle Falkoff in *The Chronicle of Higher Education*. "But if academic institutions do not take steps to assess teaching more holistically, they run the risk of losing talented faculty members for reasons that are not only inappropriate but may well be illegal." I shared this peek behind the curtain with students each semester, all along knowing that at least one, but probably more, would complain to my supervisor and score my teaching negatively both because they were upset by the course subject matter and because I am Latinx.

I shouldn't have to explain to an administrator that it's racist to allow White faculty members to raise their voices and lean in when students are intellectually dishonest or jerks but not allow Black and Brown faculty members to do so. I shouldn't have to explain that students of color are harmed when professors allow their classmates to belittle their fears or experiences with racism. I shouldn't have to explain that racists take classes clearly labeled as focusing on social justice specifically so that they can disrupt them—that it is a strategy promoted by right-wing organizations. I shouldn't have to explain that even students of color can uphold White supremacy, thanks to the hidden curriculum and other tools of whiteness. But I did have to explain all those things. That, too, was whiteness at work.

Today, public intellectuals, cable news analysts, presidential candidates, op/ed writers, celebrities and others are using their platforms to talk about the issues covered by the courses I taught at AU. They're talking about structural racism and White privilege. They're talking about the dangers of bothsidesism. They're talking about redlining, the wealth gap and health disparities. When a White man used an automatic weapon to gun down people who look like me in El Paso, they talked about the deadly consequences of Trump's rhetoric. During the Democratic primary race, they talked about why it was acceptable for Beto O'Rourke to raise his voice but disqualifying for Julián Castro or Cory Booker to raise theirs. Taylor Swift is teaching her fans, by example, what it means to be an ally. I find a modicum of comfort in knowing that hundreds of students who passed through my classes have the knowledge base and mental tools to navigate those discourses. I am saddened, though, that the students who instead signed up to read and write about food, sports and fairy tales might not.

Proceed with Caution—But Toward Justice

Would joining or starting a side program for writers of color have made my MFA experience better? Maybe. Would keeping my mouth shut, endearing myself to colleagues and attending their dinner parties have made my faculty experience better? Maybe. But it wouldn't have even begun to address the underlying problem: faculty members who refuse to recognize or reflect on their own privilege and administrators who don't have the courage to make examples of those who are out of line. So, with all due respect to Junot Díaz and others who do have the courage to expose the White supremacy in academia, let's stop advocating for workarounds and start demanding radical changes.

We've seen what happens when institutions hold those in power accountable for their actions and, importantly, inaction. At the University of Missouri, a president and a chancellor were forced to resign in 2015 after not responding appropriately to various racist incidents on campus. At San Jose State University in 2014, a vice president and a member of the board of trustees stepped down after the board member said Latinas "do not have the DNA to be successful" and the vice president failed to condemn the statement. Yale University and Brown University, both of which have had their share of discrimination fallout, pledged $50 million and $100 million to increase faculty diversity and promote inclusion, respectively (Flaherty 2016). That is the kind of change and commitment we need to see nationwide.

For those students of color applying for MFA programs and struggling through them: My advice to you is to proceed with caution but not underestimate the power you do hold. While the tenure system protects faculty members who mistreat students, you need only look to universities where student voices have brought about tremendous changes. If you're not the type to form a human blockade or chant through a bullhorn, you can make your voice heard by not signing up for classes with professors who have histories of offenses. (Ask other students of color. Trust me: These people are known quantities.) And, of course, you can write about your experiences so that others will be better prepared for what awaits them in the White MFA world.

For those faculty members who recognize this moral imperative and genuinely want to be allies: You might not get to yuck it up about how skillfully a colleague can saber a bottle of champagne at the holiday party, but you might help move us one step closer to a more just world.

Sources

Cabrera, N.L. 2012. "Exposing Whiteness in Higher Education: White Male College Students Minimizing Racism, Claiming Victimization, and Recreating White Supremacy." *Race Ethnicity and Education*. 17: 30–55. doi.org/10.1080/13613324.2012.725040.

Cabrera, N.L. 2012. "Working through Whiteness: White, Male College Students Challenging Racism." *The Review of Higher Education*. 35(3): 375–401. doi.org/10.1353/rhe.2012.0020.

Díaz, J. 2014. "MFA vs. POC." *The New Yorker*, April 30, 2014. newyorker.com/books/page-turner/mfa-vs-poc.

Falkoff, M. 2018. "Why We Must Stop Relying on Student Ratings of Teaching." *The Chronicle of Higher Education,* April 25, 2018. chronicle.com/article/Why-We-Must-Stop-Relying-on/243213.

Flaherty, C. 2016. "Beyond Well-Funded Individual Campus Initiatives, Experts Urge Collaboration on Increasing Faculty Diversity." *Inside Higher Ed*, September 19, 2016. insidehighered.com/news/2016/09/19/beyond-well-funded-individual-campus-initiatives-experts-urge-collaboration.

Hoagland, T. 2003. *What Narcissism Means to Me*. Saint Paul, Minnesota: Graywolf.

Hoagland, T. 2011. "Dear Claudia: A Letter in Response." *Academy of American Poets (poets.org)*, March 14, 2011. poets.org/text/dear-claudia-letter-response.

Hoagland, T. 2018. "The Cure for Racism is Cancer." *The Sun Magazine*, September 2018. thesunmagazine.org/issues/513/the-cure-for-racism-is-cancer.

hooks, b. 1994. *Teaching to Transgress: Education as the Practice of Freedom*. New York: Routledge.

Jacobs, J. 2018. "Junot Díaz Remains on Pulitzer Board After Review of Misconduct Allegations." *The New York Times*, November 17, 2018. nytimes.com/2018/11/16/us/junot-diaz-pulitzer-board.html.

Jaschik, S. 2014. "Following Complaint, 2 Resignations at San Jose State." *Inside Higher Ed*, November 17, 2014. insidehighered.com/quicktakes/2014/11/17/following-complaint-2-resignations-san-jose-state.

Kelley, B.J. 2018. "Turning Point USA's Blooming Romance with the Alt-Right." *Southern Poverty Law Center*, February 16, 2018. splcenter.org/hatewatch/2018/02/16/turning-point-usas-blooming-romance-alt-right.

McFadden, S. 2015. "Black Bodies in White Words, Or: Why We Need Claudia Rankine." *National Public Radio*, March 4, 2015.

npr.org/sections/codeswitch/2015/03/04/387533984/black-bodies-in-white-words-or-why-we-need-claudia-rankine.

Messner, M.A. 2000. "White Guy Habitus in the Classroom." *Men and Masculinities*. 2(4): 457–69. doi.org/10.1177/1097184x00002004005.

Moreno, M.A. 2018. "Donald Trump's Rhetoric is Going to Get Us Killed." In *Not White/Straight/Male/Healthy Enough: Being "Other" in the Academy*, edited by Michael A. Moreno, Kathryn Quinn–Sánchez and Michele Shaul. Newcastle Upon Tyne, UK: Cambridge Scholars Publishing.

Neary, L. 2014. "In Elite MFA Programs, The Challenge of Writing While 'Other'." *National Public Radio*, August 19, 2014. npr.org/sections/codeswitch/2014/08/19/341363580/in-elite-mfa-programs-the-challenge-of-writing-while-other.

O'Brien, L.T., Crandall, C.S., Horstman–Reser, A., Warner, R., Alsbrooks, A., and Blodorn, A. 2010. "But I'm No Bigot: How Prejudiced White Americans Maintain Unprejudiced Self-Images." *Journal of Applied Social Psychology*. 40(4): 917–46. doi.org/10.1111/j.1559-1816.2010.00604.x.

Parsons, K. 2009. "Caroline County Murder Victim Identified." *WBOC*, August 12, 2009. wboc.com/story/10891853/caroline-county-murder-victim-identified.

Phillips, A. 2017. "'They're Rapists.' President Trump's Campaign Launch Speech Two Years Later, Annotated." *The Washington Post*, June 16, 2017. washingtonpost.com/news/the-fix/wp/2017/06/16/theyre-rapists-presidents-trump-campaign-launch-speech-two-years-later-annotated/.

Picower, B. 2009. "The Unexamined Whiteness of Teaching: How White Teachers Maintain and Enact Dominant Racial Ideologies." *Race Ethnicity and Education*. 12(2): 197–215. doi.org/10.1080/13613320902995475.

Rankine, C. 2011. "Open Letter: A Dialogue on Race and Poetry." *Academy of American Poets (poets.org)*, February 14, 2011. poets.org/text/open-letter-dialogue-race-and-poetry.

Ritter, Z.S. 2016. "International Students' Perceptions of Race and Socio-Economic Status in an American Higher Education Landscape." *Journal of International Students*. 6(2): 367–93. files.eric.ed.gov/fulltext/EJ1094879.pdf.

Shanahan, M., and Ebbert, S. 2018. "Junot Diaz is Cleared in MIT Investigation." *The Boston Globe*, June 18, 2018. bostonglobe.com/arts/2018/06/18/junot-diaz-cleared-mit-investigation/IsxX7V90CVSPXLXuwCFZGL/story.html.

Svrluga, S. 2015. "Students Take Racist Comments and Spread Them All over Campus." *The Washington Post*, October 21, 2015. washingtonpost.com/news/grade-point/wp/2015/10/21/students-take-racist-comments-and-spread-them-all-over-campus/.

"Turning Point USA." *Anti-Defamation League*. Accessed May 30, 2020. adl.org/resources/backgrounders/turning-point-usa.

Toward Restoration and Justice: Whiteness in Higher Education and Teaching Anti-Racism

Jacqueline Lantsman

"I feel like this is supposed to make me feel bad for not having grown up around people of color or not having had Black kids in my classes," professed a White student after sitting distraughtly disengaged from a group dialogue. "What was I supposed to do growing up?" she continued. "This conversation doesn't seem fair—to benefit from something I wasn't aware of and didn't have control over. Why am I responsible for that?"

Other White students locked eyes with me, waiting and hoping to receive permission to support the student. Often my whiteness at the head of the classroom gave way to White students expecting validation. They sought permission to express their discomfort and false appeasement for their fragility.

My response to this situation wasn't to indulge such statements; however, I also did not reprimand White students. I recognized the privilege of my whiteness and the opportunity for it to act as a bridge to encourage critical analysis, productive discomfort and, the ultimate goal, a commitment to anti-racism.

In the past, my work as a peer co-teacher to a first-year student transition course was driven to answer two questions,

1. How do we incentivize those untouched by injustice to care and stand with marginalized communities?
2. How do we incentivize those who inherently benefit from injustice and marginalization to care and stand with affected communities?

However, if answering those two questions is the single focus of social justice teaching, stories of injustice and reasons to challenge systemic oppression will be framed to meet White appetite. Conversations about oppression will be made digestible, upholding the assimilationist censorship that claims intergenerational trauma cannot be portrayed as anger and protest because such portrayals are off-putting to White people. My experiences with the course will literally portray whiteness at work, both from my experience as a White woman teaching a course on race, privilege, and institutions of power, and the mechanics of a majority-White class learning about systems of oppression.

My Co-Teacher, Peer-Facilitator Role

For a year, I engaged with and challenged insecure statements made by White students who hadn't previously grappled with their contributions to and benefits from racial injustice. Twice a week, alongside my co-instructor, I facilitated a dialogue-based course dedicated to race, privilege and institutions of power. The course was mandatory for the entire first-year student body, which was predominantly White and had a median family income of $150,000. Roughly 70 percent of students belonged to families whose accrued wealth was more than 80 percent of the U.S. population's assets. In 2017, students of color consisted of just under one-third of the student population.

While my whiteness was a comfort to White students and a mechanism to make the course accessible to their learning, consistently, across the university, students and faculty were raising a question: For whom is the course intended?

While the course ostensibly existed to foster culture change and promote inclusion across campus, I wondered if the legs the course stood on were antithetical to inclusion, centering the White student, as opposed to elevating students of color?

This essay will describe course exercises, encounters I had with students, and the university climate at a predominantly White institution, all of which challenged me to consider what hinders the practice of anti-racism and future opportunities for equitable higher education.

The Cloak of Progressivism

The university is a traditional campus, with flora occupying just about every inch of the outdoor 90-acre area. In some respects, it is secluded from the intensity of D.C. politics to ensure students focus on their development as scholars and as people. However, the university thrives on contradiction, given that the student body is ranked within the top 10 of politically active, reflected in the assortment of advocacy organizations students intern for during their undergraduate careers.

Attempting to pay respects to the land the university was built on, on multiple occasions prior to the start of lecture, professors named the Native American tribes to whom the land once belonged. This ritual offered a reminder of the nation's history of violence and displacement—and attempted to practice gratitude for the soil formerly nourished by Native Americans that now serves the plant life and students. The university has long focused on imposing policy that promotes student co-existence, whether with the environment, with fellow students, or with the surrounding community—the symbolic practice of paying respect and co-existing with the land corresponds to the university's approach to diversity and inclusion.

However, while some lecturers attempt to respect the land, the administration launched an energy-saving initiative that led to the addition of an underground heating system. Intended to improve energy efficiency and sustainability, the four-year construction project overturned the earth, lifting debris into the air while workers installed insulated piping to contain the heat within from getting lost in the surrounding ground.

To have gratitude for the soil in one instance and displace it in another speaks to the hypocrisy that results from the institutional priorities and decisions by the administration around what it is willing to compromise and concede in creating infrastructural change for student comfort and cost savings.

In some instances, the university aligns itself with progressive values, such as the paying of respect to the Native Americans formerly having occupied university land, however, when the comfort of the predominantly White university body stands counter to structural change, university administrators stand shyly unsure of how to proceed. The progressive beliefs about which the university boasts are conditional. Reform toward inclusion will require compromise and discomfort by a majority-White student body and administration. As I began to teach this course, I would question whether it did enough to promote structural change or whether it conceded to the pressures of White comfortability.

The Class Itself

One of the first lessons I co-taught in the course involved developing community norms. I stood before students arriving from across the United States and abroad, establishing the importance of discussion guidelines—a method for fostering a safe learning environment where students' academic freedom is protected. The assumption was that, naturally, due to different conventions of behavior, students would offend each other. Agreed-upon expectations would presumably prevent hostility and exclusion.

While this exercise challenged students to consider how they wanted to be treated, it did not challenge them to consider what restoration or resolution would look like in the case that offense was taken and safety was suspended. A class of majority-White students was tasked with creating norms to create productive dialogue around race, privilege, and institutions of power.

At first, they were so quiet a pin could drop and an echo would reverberate throughout the room. Soon though, after one hand shot up, two consecutive palms reached for the air. The pattern persisted, and one after the other students clarified and challenged norms proposed by their classmates. Roughly half of the students offered suggestions for what was required to protect their learning.

1. Avoid generalizing a single experience you had with a person as your understanding of a whole category of people.
2. While you listen, be willing to sit with your discomfort with other people's personal experience(s).
3. Listen actively.
4. Assume positive intent on the part of fellow participants.

While guidelines were collectively agreed upon, a consensus was not reached. Students occupying the majority had greater influence over norms selection. Standing witness, I tried to identify an intervention that would elevate voices that had not been raised. The course content schedule demanded that we move forward, however, and, as the months progressed, I grappled with (1) why norms were necessary, beyond the evident geographic diversity of the student body, and (2) who the guidelines were protecting—students living with the realities of daily racial oppression or the fragile White students disturbed by the idea that their success and comfort stand atop structural racism perpetrated against nonwhite Americans and peoples abroad.

Don't Generalize

While students should treat anecdotes as stand-alone experiences rather than broad generalizations of communities so to promote personhood and agency, the "don't generalize" community norm fails to acknowledge that stereotypes possessed by those with White privilege have been weaponized historically to exclude, to oppress, to silence.

There must be a realization among administrators that, comparatively, the generalizations of White students have greater consequences. In a world where there is motivation for White individuals to morph generalizations into stereotypes to justify their compliance in oppression and protecting their power, we as educators must clearly state that ours is not a post-racial society—racial equity needs to be at the forefront of how we create community norms.

During the course, I also noticed the trend of whitewashing. When teaching implicit/unconscious bias using psychological science, which states that we are all susceptible to implicit bias due to prehistoric needs for survival, I found myself treating implicit bias as an apolitical, impartial act, evading the historic pain implicit bias is submerged under. In class, we discussed how implicit bias is informed by our circles of influence and the individuals from whom we access information.

While it's true that our circles of influence inform the origins of our beliefs and our concerns, this was when the White student I mentioned earlier, the one who expressed guilt for having grown up in a White monolithic community, made her protest of discomfort.

As I took the space to fully hear the student's sentiments, I had less space to cite research on the historic segregation, redlining, and displacement of communities of color, police interactions with students of color on college campuses—most recently exhibited by a 20-minute encounter between police and a Yale University student required to verify her status as a student because napping in a dormitory common room was considered suspicious—and the national controversy to support affinity spaces in primarily White institutions, which could highlight the privilege whiteness bares to choose where and when to occupy space.

Beyond using theoretical jargon to depoliticize tools of oppression, one of my students, a woman of color, pulled me aside at the end of class. She began to point out how generalizations operate in our teaching of oppression. When we teach about oppression, we often negate narratives that don't fit the conventional mold of marginalization. As her eyes carefully traced every student that exited the classroom, it was clear to me that this necessitated privacy. She began to explain that she doesn't know how to portray her identity at a primarily White institution. She communicated that by telling White classmates who she is—a Black, upper-middle-class immigrant who grew up in a U.S. suburb with two physician parents—she would give students skeptical of structural racial oppression a reason to discount marginal opportunities among people of color in the United States. She worried that, if her narrative defies the statistics that reveal overrepresentation of Black workers in low-wage service jobs and a median wage disparity, or if her narrative hints at home ownership in a wealthy U.S. suburb when evidence reveals historic predatory lending to African-

American homeowners and high rates of foreclosure in communities of color, it would undermine the learning outcomes of the course. She thought: The less confusion among White students, the better.

This course, and pedagogy across academia, in its attempt to teach racism and systemic oppression relies on cut-and-dry images of unfairness and statistics. While statistics embody generalizable, community-spanning consequences of racist policy, independently, statistics fail to offer examples of dynamic experiences with systems of oppression. When curriculum strictly provides drastic examples of unfairness and privilege, we neglect the stories in between. We silence students and inhibit nuanced learning. We overlook opportunities to build bridges and offer chances for students to witness commonality and develop empathy.

A more structural criticism, regarding this problem, was made by Kimberlé Crenshaw, a civil rights advocate and a leading scholar of critical race theory who coined the theory of intersectionality. Crenshaw argued that the conventional tools of thinking about oppression silo us into ascribing one explanation for injustice. In doing so, we overlook how the convergence of oppression—the simultaneous experiences people have with various policies—inform their existence. We also overlook where we can intervene to improve equitable access and opportunity. When we fail to consider the unconventional, compounding of differing systems of injustice, we postpone our development of tools to intervene in those very systems.

Thus, we must create space and encourage students to consider the role of systemic oppression that doesn't always result in outward, visible symptoms of unfairness. The stories in between have a place. Generalizable molds for oppression will not move us forward. Instead, we must challenge ourselves to think long and hard about how oppression shows itself. Anti-racist teaching is dwarfed when we center the comfortability of White students by offering cut-and-dry lessons of oppression. Generalizations used to teach about oppression at predominantly White institutions place undue pressure on students of color to authentically tell their narratives.

Seek and Sit with the Discomfort

College is often promoted as a challenging, uncomfortable opportunity for students to learn how to think critically, within the guardrails of academic freedom. However, it is worth recognizing that, while White students find comfort in primarily White institutions, students of color have very different experiences.

Discomfort for students of color is persistent, and many identify it as emotional labor. Anecdotes across institutions report how chronic incidences of hate alienate and stoke fear in students of color. Ranging from symbolic racism to threats of physical violence, the *Journal of Blacks in Higher Education* reports daily examples of racism occurring on predominantly White institutions across the United States. Ebony McGee at Vanderbilt University examines the consequences of chronic discomfort for Black students in her research. She wrote, "Weathering the cumulative effects of living in a society characterized by white dominance and privilege produces a kind of physical and mental wear-and-tear that contributes to a host of psychological and physical ailments…We have documented alarming occurrences of anxiety, stress, depression and thoughts of suicide, as well as a host of physical ailments like hair loss, diabetes and heart disease." The consequences of chronic discomfort among students of color go beyond impeding focus on immediate studies, but also have long-term effects, including decreased quality of life and higher morbidity. Given this scientific knowledge, for an institution to claim discomfort is foundational to critical thinking is not only culturally incompetent but reckless—potentially responsible for the adverse effects resulting from chronic discomfort.

When students of color seek comfort and inclusion through the creation of safe, affinity spaces, their attempts are compared to and misrepresented as re-segregationist policy. In reality, having a supportive environment where students feel heard and validated in their experiences has the capacity to counteract chronic experiences with racism and microaggressions. Across the United States, administrations fail to hear students of color.

So, I ask, who is being asked to sit with discomfort in these classrooms? Firstly, the request to become comfortable with discomfort overlooks that some students are desk-bound to the discomfort enforced by America's history of oppression, faced with it daily—while White students are more likely to be unfamiliar with conversations about injustice. For White students, to sit with discomfort is synonymous to sitting with White guilt; for students of color, sitting with discomfort in a predominantly White institution is inescapable. The request to sit with discomfort centers the White experience, prioritizing White learning. This request fails to account for the sea of microaggressions that flood the experiences of students of color—swimming with the discomfort that is required to exist at a predominantly White institution.

Listen Actively

Students in my course were assigned reading by a Black author, who centered her experiences to explain larger systemic trends of racism. This was not a commonality at the university. Most literature was written by

White scholars. Most courses were taught by White faculty. The White canon presided over the student experience in every respect. The toxicity of such power is exemplified by another comment made by a White male student in my course: "Her personal experience is not a credible, academic source. I refuse to analyze the text because it is not legitimate or suited for an academic institution." He made the comment right at the end of class, with seconds left for my co-instructor or I to craft a rebuttal explaining the critical importance of the text.

After the students exited the classroom, my co-instructor and I glared at each other in disappointment. "If a student doesn't find a Black published author credible, what type of listening and compassion does the student practice toward his fellow classmates?" I asked my co-instructor. Aware of the harm the student's comment caused to other students, potentially deterring them from sharing their personal experiences, we regrouped and considered productive steps. We held silence for five minutes. My eyes circled the floor of the classroom whose integrity for open dialogue fell to question.

We discussed the potential root cause of the sentiment. Joe Henao, author of "Linguistic Hegemony in Academia and the Devaluation of Minority Identity in Higher Education," wrote: "Hegemony determines what is proper and improper, correct and incorrect, and acceptable and unacceptable, all while effectively stifling any ideological opposition. The response to hegemony is difficult—either conform or experience marginalization." As an English-language learner—with memories of daydreaming and withdrawal from classrooms where I was asked to trace the words on a page and clap syllables—I was familiar with the concept of linguistic hegemony. To have my pronunciation and grammar consistently scrutinized, and giggles emerge among students when I failed to understand cultural references, I habitually buried my head in my hands and closed my eyes during class for years to come. My classmates were indoctrinated into a system where shaming difference and demanding conformity was normal.

What the student said to challenge the belonging of another individual's narrative in the environment of academia was "common sense" to the student—what Antonio Gramsci explains is "the success of the dominant classes in presenting their definition of reality, their view of the world." The White student used the hegemonic formula for "legitimacy" and applied it to the writing of a Black author and proceeded to conclude that he has good reason to oppose treating such text as credible. If he were to see legitimacy, his hegemonic narrative might occupy less space, might become displaced slightly in an institution that implicitly elevates his voice.

How White Hegemony Is Sustained in Academia

Are the community norms developed in the course challenging the White hegemony of a predominantly White institution or are they instead requiring conformity from students of color by prioritizing the accessibility of theoretical teachings of racial oppression to White students? Professor and philosopher Molefi Kete Asante wrote that "the rejection of European particularism as universal is the first stage of our coming intellectual struggle." It was my fear that, as I promoted the learning of a majority-White class, I was also failing to hear students of color. As a White educator in this course, I had to question how my facilitation could hinder learning—how my comfort to White students prevented me from practicing allyship and serving as a resource to students of color.

The research rung in my ears: Predominantly White institutions have been found to hamper Black students' ability to perform well academically, and attrition rates for Black students are substantially greater than those for White students.[1,2] The way in which students of color acquire justice or resolve from predominantly White institutions plays a momentous role in student success.

Particularly, the question about the accessibility of my teaching arose when we were teaching the "Good/Bad Binary," an outgrowth of the false dilemma fallacy, which uses an all-or-nothing approach to understanding a situation. When the "Good/Bad Binary"is employed, the individual's actions are categorized as either good or bad. I explained that, within the context of racism, the fallacy functions to uphold a system of absent accountability. Robin DiAngelo, a critical race scholar, argues that the binary leads us to conclude that, when someone makes an oppressive statement or commits an oppressive action, it reflects the perpetrator's moral failing. One problem with this approach is that it results in either defensiveness or dismissal. Because it takes less effort for an individual of privilege to turn away than to confront their modifiable racist ideology or behavior, our opportunity to consider what societal forces normalized such behavior—to deconstruct what information and lack of information contributed to the beliefs of the perpetrator—is thwarted. DiAngelo argues that there are dire consequences to sustaining the "Good/Bad Binary," as the construct reinforces that racism is unchangeable. Our capacity to hold White people accountable to their racism withers when we simply label White people as bad or lacking moral character.

---

[1] Allen, 1992; Fleming, 1984

[2] Guiffrida & Douthit, 2010; Cross & Slater, 2004

While, theoretically, this reframing of the consequences of racism should draw White students in, reduce their hesitation to contribute to the dialogue, and overall create a learning opportunity, when I was standing in front of students of color as the arbiter of accountability to racism I clearly wasn't prioritizing their voices. So, while the "Good/Bad Binary" is not conducive to White learning and White behavior change, who was I to stand before students of color as an arbiter of the use of a label, whose history is soaked in tremendous pain, a pain I would never feel? While, intellectually, I agree that, at a macro-level to improve accountability, we must create avenues of open dialogue to discuss wrongdoing, the instruments we use in our deliberations toward justice and restoration must be decided by those harmed by the wrongdoing. In higher education, we have avenues for doing this, however, there are roadblocks to implementation.

When a student asked, "Can we leave the classroom if we feel uncomfortable or unsafe during dialogue?" the discussion gravitated toward establishing tools students could use to sustain their personal safety and academic freedom. Soon after the question was posed, hands shot up

"Allowing students to leave the classroom would be a slippery slope."

"How are we supposed to trust that a student is actually uncomfortable instead of didn't prepare for class?"

"Getting up and leaving would be disruptive to the class."

This was normative thinking. While there was an opportunity to create instruments or pathways for an individual harmed to achieve their restoration, the system of higher education predisposes students to regulate their resolve to emotional labor. It achieves this by penalizing students, with either participation grades or social judgment.

Language of Oppression

"I don't think there is anything wrong with saying 'crazy,'" said another White student.

That was unexpected, I thought, considering how to advance our conversation about trigger warnings and use of language.

Student chatter proceeded.

"It's exhausting having to censor ourselves. So, no, I don't think there is anything wrong with the word 'crazy,'" another student plunged into the conversation, moving the tide in a direction I hadn't prepared for.

A third student chimed in, "No wonder the older generation calls us *snowflakes*. People need to stop taking offense to everything. Certain words are just more convenient to say and have been normalized in society and popular culture."

At this, my eyebrows furrowed, and my mouth cracked open. I took a slight breath, but not a single word could trust itself to confront this statement with precision.

Precision was necessary. Having become so accustomed to understanding insensitivity, the accessible, step-by-step argument I was trained to give escaped me.

"Well, why has popular culture decided that the term 'crazy' is normal when, in reality, it is offensive and stigmatizing to so many people?" I asked.

"Why is it offensive and stigmatizing?" a student murmured.

"If someone were to tell you it offended them or was insensitive to their experience with mental health, would you proceed to say it?"

With these questions, I attempted to demonstrate that we should center the individual with the experience, as opposed to the norms defined by a popular culture that gives command and power to the majority. While our acceptance of popular culture gives us the scaffolding to engage and relate with one another, we must question who was involved in the placement of bricks and who cemented the norms of our culture, and, more importantly, whose experience was left out and silenced in the weaving of this popular fabric.

The student responded, "Well, no…"

The Misrepresentation of Safe and Just Space

The four encounters I've described here raise questions about creating physical and verbal safe spaces. All also reveal a fracture in academia's capacity to prevent offense, restore justice, and serve students historically on the margins.

1. A White female student responding to housing discrimination and segregation in the United States by questioning her responsibility and culpability for encountering only white peers in school.
2. A Black student uncertain how to represent her identity in a primarily White institution.
3. A White male student invalidating the academic authority of a Black female author using her narrative to discuss structural oppression.
4. A class discussion regarding pejorative language used to describe people.

In the past and today, with the eruption of debates around censorship and academic freedom, conservative scholars question my claim that academia should prevent offense, restore justice and serve all students equitably. Bret Stephens, former dean of Yale Law School, in a 2019 opinion column for the New York Times, suggested that inclusion is analogous with anti-excellence. In his piece, he argued that the movement for inclusion, by embracing that student apprehension and concern be included in deciding what conversations and topics occupy the classroom, is a "revolt of the mediocre many against the excelled few" and that it is a system where "all are included, all are equal, all are special." Fostering inclusion by reforming what is normative and of service to White hegemonic control over higher education, Stephens implies, will strip the excellence from academia. Stephens outright equates the measure of excellence as White serving—achieved by the White monolith and by enforcement of exclusivity. Traditionally, White academics and administrators have self-interest in upholding a system that offered them career mobility. Promoting diversity and radical inclusion of students of color is at odds with those interests. While Stephens disagrees with efforts to respect and foster spaces productive for the learning of all students, when college administrators resort to traditional procedures and fail to restore justice, they sustain whiteness and exclusion.

Administrative Attempts Toward Justice and Restoration

One morning the student body woke up to a coordinated racist incident. Multiple symbols of hate were arranged around campus, with the intent of targeting students of color. Hate crimes and speech are a growing problem across the United States, with White supremacist groups growing in number and visibility. The Anti-Defamation League has found that propaganda by White supremacist groups targeting college campuses increased by 77 percent between 2017 and 2018. Of the cases included in their analysis, hate crimes based on race had spiked since 2014.[3]

Soon after investigators identified the incident on our campus as a hate crime, a student protest was organized to demand structural change. Student leaders from the Black Student Alliance and the university NAACP led the plea, describing the torment of waking up to racist symbols referencing lynching; they expressed frustration with paying tens of thousands of dollars in tuition for the wallets of administrators who refuse to make radical, anti-racist reform a priority. Cries were heard across campus and reverberated

---

[3] Anti-Defamation League. 2018. "White Supremacist Propaganda Nearly Doubles on Campus in 2017–18 Academic Year." adl.org/resources/reports/white-supremacist-propaganda-nearly-doubles-on-campus-in-2017-18-academic-year.

50 feet away in the spiritual chapel, where a town hall organized by administrators was taking place to discuss the matter. The chapel was filled to the brim with students and staff, and campus leaders attempted to provide details of the situation, direct students to support-staff offering counseling, and elevate voices in the audience by selectively offering the microphone to students who wanted to share their commentary.

During the townhall, the last university representatives to speak were the university police. They outlined two strategies to prevent such incidents from occurring again and rectify matters before students encounter the blatant racism.

1. Strategically situating surveillance across the campus to track suspicious individuals who don't match the "normal" student profile.
2. Increasing the number of officers who monitor the campus and routinely check student identification cards.

The university's main resource for rectifying violence and promoting justice was a tool that across the country was being scrutinized for its own racism—for racially profiling and committing brutality on people of color. On this note, the townhall ended.

As administrators exited the chapel to chants from the student protesters, their prepared remarks were not of service to them. A White associate dean managed to find her way to the center of a circle of protestors. The predominantly Black student crowd spoke out about the routine harm racism has on learning and about their security and safety. The protesters also brought up disingenuous attempts by administrators to include Black student organizations in discussions about program structure and curriculum development for the course I would teach only two years later.

Managing to get a megaphone handed to her, the dean stood front and center and spoke softly: "In this moment, I don't know what you're asking; I cannot do [what you want], but I can tell you, I hear it, I believe it, and I will work to implement the change."

Protestors were expected to assume positive intent on the part of the administrator; in that moment, they were asked to believe that the administrator would offer her best effort in implementing change. But how can a university leader attempt to resolve a problem she doesn't fully understand? More specifically, when administrators don't understand the desired "ask" of the student body they are attempting to serve, shouldn't they first ask and actively listen, by passing the megaphone to let student pain fester and manifest itself into blueprints for change?

Just as the university was eager to align itself with environmental values and improve its comfortability by ripping out historic piping to lay the groundwork and dedicate a long four years to reconstruction, are university leaders willing to make changes to the racially unjust social infrastructure the university stands on? When heat doesn't warm certain buildings on campus; when water doesn't reach certain residence halls, reform is made a priority. Well, then, when the bones of an institution don't serve students of color academically, or protect their physical and emotional health, what investment for reconstruction will leaders make?

Anti-Racist Attempts Toward Justice and Restoration

To foster a culture of anti-racism, inclusion and radical accountability that serves students of color, educators must find a model that can promote learning, but, first and foremost, lead with equity—center the standpoint of the individual with direct experience.

An anti-racist exercise that can be used to intervene during moments of wrongdoing is the practice of restorative justice. Rejecting the traditional adversarial system that champions draconian and retributive practices—whose origins are that of intentional dominion and control over Black Americans as enshrined by the 13th Amendment, which states "Neither slavery nor involuntary servitude, except as a punishment for crime whereof the party shall have been duly convicted, shall exist within the United States"—restorative justice offers the chance to assess who state-determined definitions of "safety" and "protection" serve. Attempting to realign the concepts of accountability and safety, by focusing on the individual pained by an encounter, the offender, and the surrounding community, restorative justice can function within academic environments.

Across the United States, restorative justice is found in the K–12 setting, where it functions as an intervention to suspension and expulsion. The literature on the school-to-prison pipeline challenged teachers and school administrators to consider alternatives to student accountability, while also fostering an effective and safe learning environment for all students. Minna Kim, a community organizer advocating for facilitating exercises like victim–offender mediation and peacemaking circles, explains that, during dialogue, students work toward "grounding [themselves] in shared values and agreements where [they] can start to talk about the wounds, the pains, that have been sitting there for so long."

While some school districts have reservations about restorative justice due to inconsistencies in research evaluating the effectiveness of the practice, the results of said experiments are attributed to differences in implementation, training variability, and the specific context of the school population. Jeff Latimer, Craig Dowden and Danielle Muise conducted a systematic literature review of existing evidence-based research on restorative justice and found that restorative justice is an effective alternative to intervening in student misbehavior.[4] In any given reform to traditional policy, administrators should monitor and facilitate opportunities for feedback from stakeholders to determine whether the intervention serves their community. With the implementation of restorative justice exercises, administrators should distribute climate surveys attempting to gauge the effectiveness of the practice.

While restorative justice in K–12 functions so that teachers and leaders reduce the physical removal of students, in higher education the exclusion and marginalization faced by students of color has equally dire consequences—decreased rates of graduation and emotional labor have potential consequences of impeding future economic mobility. This should shake the core of traditional academia to consider routes for developing radical accountability to racism while upholding the academic freedom of all students.

While I simply asked my student, "If someone were to tell you it offended them, would you proceed to say it?" restorative justice brings this question to life by creating mediated space for both parties to express their feelings about the offense and move toward resolving the conflict with their own unique understanding of justice.

Now, I want to emphasize that this mediated space is not intended for students to attempt to justify racist or oppressive remarks. The facilitator is responsible for (1) receiving agreement from both or multiple parties that their interaction will be respectful and sincere and (2) introducing what I believe is the founding idea to teaching about race, privilege, and institutions of power: Discrimination is the outgrowth of economic and political systems that indoctrinate White people to sustain behaviors that will bring them closer to supposed mobility and security in the United States, an argument made by Ibram X. Kendi in his book *Stamped from the Beginning*. Administrators recognizing and vocalizing that the foundations of the university—whether the water, piping, mechanics of heating student dorms, or curriculum on race, privilege, and institutions of power—are all the outgrowth of the decisions by leaders to oppress, whether directly or indirectly, communities of color, for White prosperity, lays the context for further discussion.

---

[4] Latimer, J., Dowden, C. & Muise, D. 2005. "The Effectiveness of Restorative Justice Practices: A Meta-Analysis." *The Prison Journal*, 85(2), 127–144. doi:10.1177/0032885505276969

These two core principles, established within a mediated restorative-justice setting, offer students involved in a harmful experience the agency to discuss:

1. personal experiences within the complex context of White supremacy;
2. the occupation of whiteness in space, language, and norms of behavior;
3. and the indoctrination of White students, and all students for that matter, to uphold systems of oppression.

In doing so, we offer a platform to students with the experience of injustice to become the arbiters—to take the space to develop anti-racist norms that restore what justice means to them. In this way, we center students of color, while including White students and helping them see their role in the restoration of justice and safety, necessary for equitable student learning at a primarily White institution.

Restorative justice can show how a single incident exemplifies the cementation of White supremacy and offer students the capacity to disrupt the levers that reinforce racism. While the community norms developed on the first day of class are well-intentioned, it isn't enough to not offend. It isn't enough "not" to be racist. Taking the next step is involving restorative justice, which takes an anti-racist approach by operating with the understanding that White supremacy is present, active, and incentivizes daily oppression. Moving beyond prevention, to active disruption and the creation of just space, is the commencement of uprooting whiteness in academia.

CONTRIBUTORS

Mark E. Attucks Sr. has more than 30 years of experience in the military, corporate and federal sectors. He has held various positions within security and resource protection, financial management, human capital management, diversity and equal employment opportunity, administration, logistics, and facility maintenance. He is currently the deputy director for operations and funds control at the U.S. Department of Justice, where he oversees in excess of $30 billion. He has a degree in legal studies and soon will begin law school at Western Michigan University.

Dennard Dayle is a Jamaican-American writer and comedian with an MFA in fiction from Columbia University and a bachelor's in English from Princeton University. His writing has appeared in *Clarkesworld*, *McSweeney's Internet Tendency*, *The Hard Times*, *Matchbook*, various other journals and anthologies, and his personal site, See More Evil.

Jaime Antonio Rivera Flores is an assistant professor of world languages and cultures at Georgian Court University in New Jersey. He holds a bachelor's degree in communication sciences and techniques from La Universidad de Xalapa, a master's in recreation administration from Georgia Southern University, and both a master's in Spanish literature and linguistics and a Ph.D. in Spanish linguistics from Florida State University. He served as first-year Spanish supervisor at the University of Tennessee from 2011 to 2013. He has led several study-abroad trips to Spain. As a writer, he has published poems and a play entitled "Adiós Mundo Cruel." He has presented his scholarly work at academic conferences in Mexico, the United States, Ecuador and Peru. His research interests include 20th century and contemporary Latin American literature. His latest scholarly article deals with an alternative origin theory to a well-known Julio Cortázar short story. In ongoing research projects, he is studying Venezuelan-born author Naida Saavedra and the New Latino Boom.

Lucía Galleno Villafán is an interdisciplinary associate professor of Spanish in the World Languages Department at Queens University of Charlotte. Her studies in languages, the humanities, the arts, and social sciences support her interest in aesthetics, writing, and civic engagement in the Charlotte area and abroad. Galleno's current research is on opera in Latin America. Galleno received her Ph.D. in Romance languages and literature with a designated emphasis in film from the University of California, Berkeley. She earned a master's degree in organizational development from Queens University of Charlotte and master's in counseling in education and mental health. Her B.A. is in linguistics and literature from the Pontificia Universidad Católica del Perú.

Jacqueline Lantsman is a graduate student in health policy at the Milken Institute School of Public Health at George Washington University. She earned her bachelor's in public health at American University and double-minored in education studies and criminal justice. Working at the intersection of three disciplines, Lantsman is involved in quantitative and qualitative research that aims to understand policy interventions to poverty alleviation broadly, with a specific focus on violence, substance abuse, and the effect of legal policy on quality of life. Lantsman has been honored for her academic scholarship by the SOPHE Vivian Drenckhahn Scholarship Award and the Gallagher Student Health Career Scholarship. She writes for the Harvard Law School Charles Hamilton Institute for Race and Justice and serves as an advocacy, equity and policy fellow with the Education Trust, a higher education policy organization that advocates for the achievement of students of color living in poverty.

Michael A. Moreno is a D.C.-area writer. He has taught first-year writing, writing and critical thinking, research writing and business writing at American University, University College University of Maryland, and the Bard College Clemente Course in Humanities at the Latin American Youth Center. He earned his MFA in creative writing from American University and bachelor's in English from the University of Houston. His scholarship, teaching and creative work focus on identity, disparities and racism. He has given talks and workshops on diversity and inclusion, privilege and allies. He tweets at @morenoreads. He has published poems, short stories and essays. Two of his pieces have been nominated for Pushcart prizes. He co-edited the anthology *Not White/Straight/Male/Healthy Enough: Being "Other" in the Academy* (Cambridge Scholars, 2018). Links to his work are available at www.michaelamoreno.com.

Luisa Kay Reyes has had pieces featured in *The Raven Chronicles*, *The Windmill*, *The Foliate Oak*, *The Eastern Iowa Review* and other literary magazines. Her essay "Thank You" was the winner of the April 2017 memoir contest of *The Dead Mule School of Southern Literature*. And her

Christmas poem was a first-place winner in the 16th Annual Stark County District Library Poetry Contest. Additionally, her essay “My Border Crossing” received a Pushcart Prize nomination from the Port Yonder Press. Two of her essays have been nominated for the “Best of the Net” anthology. One of her essays was recently featured on “The Dirty Spoon” radio hour.

Javier Sánchez is an associate professor of Spanish at Stockton University in New Jersey. He received his Ph.D. in comparative literature from the University of North Carolina at Chapel Hill. In addition to his book *Constructing Meaning in the Spanish and French New Novel: Juan Benet and Alain Robbe-Grillet* (2009), Sánchez’s articles have appeared in peer-reviewed journals such as *Dissidences: Hispanic Journal of Theory and Criticism*, *L’Érudit franco-espagnol*, *Ojáncano*, *Letras Hispanas*, *MIFLC Review* and *Hispanic Studies Review*.

tano rubio is a poet and teacher in East Tennessee. tano rubio is a pseudonym that is derived from the author’s grandparents who immigrated to the United States via the Mexican border several generations ago. He is a first-generation graduate from Lee University, with a master’s degree in teaching. He has been teaching high school English language arts for five years and is a nonfiction reader for Orison Books out of Asheville, North Carolina.

Stephanie Williams obtained her master’s in forensic psychology from the Chicago School of Professional Psychology and her Ph.D. from Palo Alto University. She has worked in the field of forensic psychology for over 14 years, most recently working as a program director for a state-funded outpatient forensic mental health clinic. She specializes in suicide risk, forensic evaluations and personality assessment of ethnic minorities. She has several peer-reviewed publications and book chapters that focus on improving mental health treatment for people of color and women. She has a private practice in the Bay Area that provides therapeutic interventions for BIPOC (Black, Indigenous and People of Color) and public safety professionals.